Sustainable Home Living and Business Magic

Green living ideas
for a sustainable home life
and home business
because Earth Day is Everyday!

Gillian Carr

Table of Contents

Living a green and sustainable life is crucial to so many people: if you are reading this book, I believe that you are a caring and protective person. Like me, you want the best for you and your family. We are seeking a healthier and less selfish way to go about our lives. When the environment around us is healthier, you and your family can actually become healthier as well.

In this book, we will take you through things you can do to improve your life by moving towards a greener life. The topics we will cover will lead you to solutions that will help improve your environment and your peace of mind. The goal here is not to add to environmental destruction but rather to create a positive relationship between you and the environment. That is where the magic lies: are meant to work together with our world, and when we do that, amazing things happen. Your contribution to making the world better is magic, and I can guarantee that you will feel that magic as you continue moving in the right direction.

The benefits will not only be for the environment, but they will impact you personally as well. Living a greener, more conscious life means living healthier, living happier, saving money: it could even make you money. Yup, you read that right, you have the opportunity to better your life in multiple aspects.

Environmental opportunities have increased since more and more people are choosing a more environmentally conscious lifestyle. That means both individuals and businesses are looking for greener solutions. If you take advantage of that, you can provide the solutions that they would benefit from, either by seeking out a green job or creating one for yourself. That could indeed lead to you earning more money for yourself while acting sustainably. Even if you are not interested in getting out there and providing solutions, you can still save money by implementing environmentally-conscious standards in your own life.

You will find everything you need in this book to kickstart your green journey. Whether you just want a greener lifestyle for you and your family or want to tap into the money-making and business benefits of going green, you will find the guidance you need. All the information you need to live a greener life, save money on food, grow beautiful and healthy gardens, and live a healthier life, you'll find in this book's pages!

More than ever, we as a society need to make a change. The environment is under strain, and we do not know how much longer we can go on like this. We all play a part in either improving our environment or degrading it, so let's be part of something that makes the world more beautiful rather than destroying it. We all have decisions to make, and our choices have consequences, even if we do not see them immediately. We are currently living with the effects that the generations that came before us have made. Let our story be one of creating a better world for ourselves and for the generations to come. It doesn't take much; we need only to decide to make a difference and then the resolve to act upon it.

If you have gotten this far, I'm assuming you will start living a more sustainable life! Let's get started on a journey that will lead to a healthier environment, a healthier life, and maybe even financial growth for you as well. There is no point in waiting any longer; let's dig in!

Chapter 1:
Starting Indoors

The first step in the journey to sustainable living is in your own home. The changes you make at home will help make you more conscious about your everyday living and help you pick up solutions to other sustainability challenges. It is a way of conditioning yourself to think sustainably and make sure you make a better change. The joy of living sustainably is not only found in doing something good for the environment, but what it does for each of us as well. Making changes to our homes in favor of sustainability also means changing our lives for the better.

When thinking of bringing sustainability in your everyday indoor living, there are many things you can do. You have the freedom to get creative and explore new ideas as often as you would like. To give you a nudge in the right direction, I have put together a few suggestions that will help you create a sustainable living space indoors.

Improving Indoor Air Quality with Plants

Our individual living spaces are not free from contamination from outside sources. Unless you live on a farm or a large plot of land, the chances are that you are in very close proximity to your neighbors and other people living around you. While community living provides certain benefits, it also means that other people's actions can affect you too, especially if you live in a city, other crowded areas, or near factories.

Air travels, which means any pollutants and toxic chemicals can travel great distances to where you are. Although reducing your impact, such as your automobile emissions is essential, there are some aspects that you cannot change on your own. However, the air quality in your space is your responsibility. There are measures that you can take to make sure that the air you breathe is clean and free from harmful chemicals.

Having plants in your indoor space is probably the best way to improve air quality. Plants take in CO_2 as well as many harmful toxins in the air and release oxygen. A study done by NASA suggests that having one plant per 100 square meters in your home or office significantly improves the air quality in the space around you (Pinola, 2015). Of course, not all plants are created equal, so you want to make sure you choose plants that maximize those benefits. A list of plants that act as air filters are:

- Chinese Evergreen
- Gerbera Daisy
- Money Plant
- Snake Plant (Mother-In-Law's Tongue)
- Areca Palm
- Dwarf Date Palm
- Boston Fern
- Kimberly Queen Fern
- Spider Plant
- Devil's Ivy
- Flamingo Lily
- Florists Chrysanthemum
- Bamboo Palm
- Weeping Fig

There are many more plants that could be useful for helping to remove toxins from the air, but this list gives you a great selection from which to choose! According to The Lung Health Institute (2016), the first five plants on this list are the best plants for increasing the oxygen in your space. Adding more plants to your living space could help you if you have been suffering from a breathing issue, or if you always feel like you need more oxygen than you are getting. All the listed plants will help remove any pollutants in your space, which may cause itchy eyes and other allergy problems. Adequate oxygen supply is essential for a healthy life, so you must take steps to have the best possible air quality around you.

Green Cleaning

Many cleaning products may get the job done, but they are not "clean" in the green sense. Modern cleaning products contain chemicals and toxins that, when released, are both terrible for the environment and our health as well. Products with a strong ammonia smell should be avoided as much as possible. Many of these products also contain artificial scents to mask the smell of those toxins, but these scents can also have some adverse health effects.

With all the negatives surrounding cleaning products, what is the right way to get your house spotless without using modern chemical cleaners? The answer is green cleaning. There are a variety of commercial cleaners available on the market that are far better for you and the environment: you can also use homemade recipes and make your own cleaning products. Try out a few and see what works for you and your home.

Many of the homemade recipes require everyday ingredients that I'm pretty sure grandma used to use. These recipes are accessible and cheaper than the regular cleaning products you usually get from the store. Before you embark on your homemade cleaner journey, make sure you have the following in your cupboard: baking soda, vinegar, lemon juice, olive oil, castile soap, and sodium carbonate (washing soda). These products will provide you with everything you need to clean your house from top to bottom. For example, a mixture of olive oil and vinegar makes the perfect wood surface cleaner. A few tablespoons of vinegar diluted with 3 cups of water will make an ideal window cleaner. Baking soda and vinegar make for a good bathroom cleaner and can be used to scrub down tiles.

Even though these products are outstanding cleaners, they are not as strong as chemical cleaners. That does mean that you will be using a bit more elbow grease to remove stubborn dirt. Green commercial cleaners help with this and take out the mixing and measuring factor of the at-home recipes. So, in addition to making your concoctions, or to save you time, green cleaners can generally be found at your local store, and there are usually quite a few brands available.

The most challenging thing to clean in a house is probably the oven. For the most part, the bottom of the range is what gets dirtiest, since oils and debris from food get stuck to it. Try placing a piece of aluminum foil or a baking tray at the bottom of your oven to catch any drips and spills. This way, the foil can be removed and thrown away when dirty, or the tray can be soaked in hot water and washed.

In general, you should try and avoid air fresheners; they have chemicals in them that can disrupt the hormones in our bodies (Lallanilla, 2019). If there is a particular area in your house that needs a fresher scent, try fresh flowers or a naturally scented candle. Baking soda can also absorb unpleasant odors: just place a small bowl of it in the corner of the area you would like to remove the smell from, and it should do the trick. Last but not least, always remember to open your windows once a day and keep them open as much as possible: this is the best way to get fresh air in your house.

Water and Power Use

Reducing the amount of water and power you use is one of the best ways to live sustainably. Both the process of treating water ready for us to use and producing energy can have massive environmental impacts. The truth is that most of us don't need to use as much water and power as we do: we have just so become accustomed to the convenience of having it right at our fingertips that we no longer think about how they are delivered to us.

There are plenty of ways that we can all save water. If you make conscious water choices, you can end up saving gallons of water throughout the month. The first thing you should do is make sure that none of your pipes or faucets are leaking: you would be surprised at how much water you can waste through leaks. Instead of washing the dishes with the tap running, fill the sink with water and use that. You can also reuse water; for instance, if you used water to rinse your vegetables or rice, you can reuse it to water your plants. If you can, install a water meter: it will help you keep track of and only pay for the water you use.

Installing a water filtration system in our homes holds massive benefits for you and the environment. Usually, once we have used water, it goes down the drain, and it's not our problem anymore, with the resulting massive waste. Most of the water that goes down the drain can be reused after a little filtering: this is the purpose of a water filtration system. The system cleans and recycles the water so that it is ready for you to use again. Water filtration is entirely safe and uses the same or similar cleaning processes as the water sources that provide water for the town or city where you live. This type of filtration is a sustainable, inexpensive, and environmentally friendly way to conserve water.

Watch how much water you are using when you bathe or shower: for many years, people thought that showering wasted less water than baths, but this depends on a few factors. If you shower longer than seven minutes, the chances are you are wasting water. If you occasionally have a long and relaxing bath, fill up the tub, and have a great soak in there! You will not have the water running for long periods as with a shower, and it is also then possible to reuse the tub water for other things, like filling your toilet tank with it or using it to water your garden. If you are planning on watering your garden with the bathwater, you should be aware that some plants take to it better than others, so you should always test a small area first to see how your plants will react. To be on the safe side, water your lawn and ornamental plants (non-food producing plants) with the bathwater and direct it at the roots, not on the leaves (Clark, 2007).

Saving power is just as crucial as conserving water. Significant work and resources go into creating electricity for a community, so the more you use, the more strain you place on the production system. Many power-saving changes do not require much effort or attention at all. In fact, there are a few quick swaps that can make a big difference. This can also help you save a bit in your bank account: if you use less electricity, your bills will be lower, amazing!

Swapping certain products with their energy-efficient counterparts is one of the easiest ways to conserve energy. Instead of using regular or CFL light bulbs, swap them out for LED bulbs: these last about 90% longer and do not release harmful gases. Instead of washing your clothes with hot water, use the cold water setting on your washing machine. This may well be better for your clothes in the long run; if you do have a tough stain on an item of clothing, just soak it in hot water and detergent before tossing it into the machine. Simply switching off the various device's power can make a huge difference: make a habit of switching off or unplugging the appliances and other devices. Another tip that people usually don't think of is merely opening up the curtains. Letting natural light in your house reduces the need to switch on your lights. These are effortless and efficient ways to save power in your everyday life.

Be mindful of where your power is coming from: some power sources are much better for the environment than others. Fossil fuels such as coal and oil are probably the worst for the environment because they release pollutants as they create energy, and are non-renewable, so once they are gone, they are gone for good. Nuclear power is a common way of creating energy for many countries; however, it creates a lot of waste. Nuclear waste is a major problem, and scientists are still trying to figure out how to dispose of it safely.

Do some research on how the government provides energy for your area. If it is fossil fuels or nuclear power, perhaps you can look at ways of creating your own energy to lessen your environmental impact. There are multiple ways in which energy can be created: hydropower and wind energy are two of them. Many cities and towns have already adopted these methods, but it can be difficult for you to do that on your own. The best form of energy you can switch to on your own would undoubtedly be solar power. If you live in a place that has an abundance of sunlight, this is obviously a great option. It may sound like a big expense to install the solar panels when you first get bids, but this is a one-time charge for a long-term saving of both energy and money. Many, if not all, power companies have incentives, and a monthly payment option is available for most homeowners. These incentives and financing plans make it easy and would likely be very affordable for you! Isn't it time to make the call?

Indoor Climatization (Heating and Cooling)

We all want our living spaces to be comfortable, which is why we have heating and cooling systems installed in our homes and offices. However, these systems can use up a lot of unnecessary power and can be harmful to the environment. You will be glad to know that you can still be comfortable and live sustainably with just a few tweaks.

Invest in a smart thermostat: this will help you to control the temperature of your house from wherever you are. Once you have installed it, you will be able to change settings directly from your smartphone with an app. Switching to a smart thermostat can save you about 50% on your electricity bill because you have complete control of when and how the thermostat works. When you are away during the day or even for longer periods, you do not need the heating or air conditioning running, so you have the option of turning them off and switching them back on before you return home. It is a smart way of staying comfortable and saving electricity.

If you have an air filter or an air cleaning system, make sure that it is maintained and cleaned out regularly. These will end up working a lot harder for little output if they are not maintained properly, so you may feel as though the air around you is the same as it always is, but the machine may be working harder. Try checking up on it every few months, clean it out, and see how much more efficiently it runs.

Sometimes it may not even be the air conditioning system that is the problem but rather how everything is arranged in your rooms. Before you pump up the aircon, do a quick check around your space and see if your furniture could block the airflow. If so, it's time for a rapid reorganization. There should be nothing stopping the air going into or coming from your heat or cooling vents to maximize your living space's efficiency.

Lastly, natural heating and cooling are always better. If there is a way for you to use what nature has already given you to control the temperature, then do it. For instance, open up the curtains and close the windows to allow some heat to enter. Or if the room is too hot because of the sun, open up the window and use heavy curtains to block out the direct sunlight. If it is at all possible, choose to spend your time around the house where the temperature is most favorable naturally. That may not be possible for everyone, but you may enjoy lower electricity use and expense if you are able.

Chapter 2:
Taking the Green Home Outdoors

We have discussed how to make your indoor living space greener and more eco-friendly, but what about the outdoors? Our outdoor areas can be easily forgotten because, well, it's outdoors. We can make our home more sustainable by creating beautiful eco-friendly outdoor entertainment areas and gardens. From painting your outside-facing walls to improving your outdoor entertainment areas, there are plenty of things you can do to make your house run more efficiently.

Rainwater Harvesting

Rainwater harvesting has been used for many years as a way to conserve water and use the water that is already freely available to us. It is an environmentally conscious act and can save you money as well.

What is Rainwater Harvesting?

Rainwater capture is the collection of the water that falls freely from the sky for the use at home

(Green Education Foundation, n.d.). This water can be used for various purposes around the house, such as watering the garden, flushing the toilet, and even cleaning the house. It should not be used as drinking water unless it can go through approved cleaning measures and filtration processes.

Water is a precious resource, and we need it to live. Unfortunately, the overuse of this resource is a reality in today's society. There is limited water available, so when we overuse it, we are pulling it from other sources that also need it. We see this in the changing landscape and many water sourcing challenges in California and elsewhere. Farmers VS the cities and development; it is quite a problem in many areas. Rainwater harvesting is a great solution since we are not pulling the freshwater from other sources but using what is already available.

Rainwater can be collected in barrels outside the house and then used when needed. Rainwater from rooftops is commonly collected and is then directed via the gutters into the storage tanks. Once the water is in the tank, you are free to use it whenever you like. It is low maintenance and low effort.

Benefits of Rainwater Harvesting

Rainwater harvesting has many benefits for both you and the environment. It allows you to be self-sufficient as you do not need to rely on the municipality's water (or well water). Instead, you use the water landing on your home and lessen your environmental footprint by placing less pressure on dams that provide the vast majority of people with water.

Even if you are not keen on purchasing a filtration system and would rather not use rainwater for drinking purposes, rainwater harvesting still has many water conservation benefits. In whatever capacity you are using it, you will still be conserving water. It will allow you to become more conscious about how you use and how much water you use regularly. If your community relies on imported water for your water provision, this will reduce the amount of water needed to be transported to your area. Rainwater can also provide an excellent backup for emergencies that may cause you to lose access to your water supply.

Rainwater harvesting also comes with many benefits for the environment. When it rains, water runs off the ground surface and picks up many chemicals and other pollutants. These pollutants are then carried off into large water sources such as dams and lakes: this is a significant cause of pollution. Collecting the rainwater lessens the amount of run-off that occurs. It also helps with stormwater management in a municipality. Rainwater is also a better source of water for plants because it does not have any chemicals added to it: keeping hold of rainwater means that you can water your garden even when it hasn't been raining for a while.

There are even economic benefits to rainwater harvesting. For you, it saves you money on your water bill since you are not relying on the municipality to provide you with water. Suppose a large number of people in the municipality or town are using rainwater harvesting for some of their water needs. In that case, this greatly decreases the pressure put on the municipality to provide water. They will not have to build new infrastructure to keep up with the water demand. Instead, what is already built can be used and maintained. The money saved can be redirected into other resources. Rainwater collection can also create jobs, as the filters and barrels need to be designed, produced, and installed.

Collecting Rainwater in Different states

There are no states where rainwater capture is entirely illegal. Some states do have stricter laws and regulations regarding it, but you may still be able to collect yours if you follow the guidelines and know the restrictions put in place. If you do live in a state that has strict rainwater harvesting regulations, do your research to make sure that you are complying with your local laws. Below is a list of states where rainwater capture is encouraged, legal, and legal with restrictions, as provided by World Population Review (2020):

Encouraged:

- Connecticut
- Delaware
- Florida
- Hawaii
- Indiana
- Maryland
- Massachusetts
- Michigan
- Minnesota
- Mississippi
- Missouri
- Montana
- Nebraska
- New Hampshire

- New Mexico
- New York
- North Dakota
- Pennsylvania
- Rhode Island
- South Carolina
- Virginia

Legal:

- Alabama
- Alaska
- Arizona
- Iowa
- Kansas
- Kentucky
- Maine
- New Jersey
- Oklahoma
- South Dakota
- Tennessee
- Vermont
- Washington

- West Virginia
- Wisconsin
- Wyoming

Legal with restrictions:

- Arkansas
- California
- Colorado
- Georgia
- Idaho
- Illinois
- Louisiana
- Nevada
- North Carolina
- Ohio
- Oregon
- Texas
- Utah

If you are reading this after 2020, please be sure to check your state's stance on rainwater capture, as it might have been updated.

Steps for Rainwater Harvesting

You might be interested in rainwater harvesting but may not know where to start. The following steps provided by Elemental Green (n.d.) will guide you along the process so you can get the most out of rainwater harvesting:

1. Make sure that the surface of the roof of your house is suitable for water collection. The best roof surfaces for this are steel sheets, well fired glazed tiles, concrete or cement tiles, clay tiles, and composite tiles. These surfaces are less likely to deposit harmful substances into your water. If you want to use the water for drinking and cooking purposes, you need to contact the manufacturer of the roofing surface or an expert to confirm that it will be safe.

2. Take a look at your gutters and make sure they are meeting the standards and regulations for your area. It is important to keep your gutters well maintained and cleaned as they can be a breeding ground for bacteria and mosquitoes. Certain fungi might also grow on them because of the moist environment. Regular checking and cleaning are required to make sure your gutters are in top form.

3. Install a gutter mesh system, which must be fireproof. The mesh system will prevent any debris, leaves, and any other larger materials from landing in the gutter and getting stuck. The weave of the mesh must not be too fine as there needs to be enough sunlight coming through the mesh. If it is too fine, there is a risk that spiders will make their homes in the shade it provides, and we definitely do not want spiders in our water.

4. Install gutter outlets, which will help prevent the pooling of water and minimize sludge buildup. Fit them to the underside of the gutter so that there is no obstruction to the water flow.

5. Fit rain heads onto the downpipes of your gutters. The rain heads direct leaves and other larger debris away from the water flow, catching them and preventing them from falling into your storage container. The container will need to be cleaned out every so often to prevent excessive buildup. Two types of containers can be installed, the type that catches the buildup into a junk basket, and the type that screens it onto the ground. The second type will require less effort and clean up from you.

6. Install insect-proof screens to all pipe entrances and exits. It is important to protect your water from insects, especially mosquitoes. Bugs can carry with them many bacteria that can cause illnesses, so it is wise to prevent contamination. These screens should still allow oxygen in and out, so make sure they are vented. Allowing the air in and out will also make sure that you do not create a vacuum in your system.

7. Install first flush water diverters. This will prevent the first rush of water from entering your tank: the water that has picked up dirt and other things from the roof. It will be the most unclean water, and it is best to have that washed away. The volume of water that will be diverted will be determined by the size of the roof and the amount of pollution in your area. The type of water diverter you will need will be subject to the kind of gutter and piping system you have installed. Once that water has been diverted, the cleaner water will then be allowed into the tank.

8. Select your water tank. The tank you need will be determined by your needs and how much water you will be expecting to use. You will also need to consider the amount

of rainfall in your area and the catchment size of your roof. There are many different tanks to choose from, so do some research and see what is available in your area. Tank top-up and pump systems will also vary, so you will need to decide whether you would like the one that automatically tops up.

9. If you are looking to use the water you have collected for indoor purposes, you should draw the aerobic zone's water. The aerobic zone provides the best quality water and is located closer to the tank's top as this water has better exposure to air circulation. If you are planning on using the water for indoor use, you should also get a tank that has two outtake points, one at the top and one at the bottom. Water taken from the bottom of the tank can be used for watering the garden and other outside uses.

10. Make sure you maintain your system well. Even the world's best systems lose efficacy over time as pipes get old, and even the best designs eventually get worn out. Your job is to ensure that your system runs the best it can: remember that regular maintenance will save you money down the line. Waiting too long between

maintenance checks can lead to permanent damage and breakages. It's best to fix something small now than waiting for it to become a bigger problem down the line. Get a professional to guide you on how often your system and tanks need to be serviced. That is dependent on the type of system you have and how much work it is asked to perform.

Regulating Your House Temperature

Many factors affect your house's indoor temperature and some of these are linked to the outside of your house. We want our houses to be comfortable to live in and temperature plays a big factor in comfort. However, many of the 'normal' ways of regulating temperature are just not good for the environment and end up using a lot of power. The good news is that there are a few things you can do to help make your house more comfortable without using excess energy.

The color of your house is an important factor to consider. Most of the time when people look to paint their houses, they are looking for a color that is fashionable and will be aesthetically pleasing to look at. However, there is more to consider when picking the color for the outside of your house.

Certain colors retain heat and others reflect heat, this is important to consider when looking for a color for your house. Darker colors absorb heat and keep it within the walls, this results in the temperature of the inside of the house rising. If you live in a colder climate and want a warmer house look for darker colors, as the heat retention can be over 70%. Lighter colors reflect the heat from the sun, so this is a good option for warmer climates. Lighter colors reflect about 35% more heat than darker colors, this will help in bringing the temperature of your house down. If you aren't a fan of light colors, opt for cooler tones like blues and greens as they are also more effective at blocking solar radiation.

The next thing you should consider is what your house is made of, as the building materials of your house can play an important factor in the temperature inside. This is obviously not something that's easy to change if you are already happy and settled into your home, but if you are planning on moving, consider this when picking your next home.

Buildings made out of denser materials such as brick and concrete are much better at regulating temperature than lightweight wall material such as wood and drywall. These denser materials help the house stay warmer in cooler temperatures and cooler in warmer temperatures. The reason for this is that brick and concrete hold on to the heat from the sun for much longer, releasing it slowly into the house. This process of holding onto the heat allows the warming of the house to slow down in hotter temperatures and the cooling of the house to slow down in colder temperatures.

These materials can also help with making sure your house is at a comfortable temperature at different times of the day. During the day, when the sun is out and it is hot out, the walls will soak up the heat and since it takes a while for it to release into the house, the interior will stay cooler during the day. As the day progresses, the heat will be released so that you will have a warmer house during the cooler nights.

Composite Decking

Composite decking is a great choice for those who love the look of a wooden deck but want something more manageable and eco-friendly. These decks are made up of recycled wood and plastic chips, which are all bonded together with a bonding agent. Using recycled material is what makes this sort of decking eco-friendly and sustainable.

While composite decking can be expensive as an initial purchase, it is a much lower maintenance option than wooden decking. Wood decking has to be touched up at least once a year since it tends to splinter and the varnish quickly loses its shine. You do not need to worry about that with composite decking: a quick wash with some soap and water twice a year should keep it looking brand new for many years. There is no risk of splinters or nails sticking out so you are free to walk around barefoot as much as you like: this also makes it a much safer option for the kids.

You can find composite decking in a variety of colors and shades to suit almost all styles and preferences. Some even mimic rare types of wood that you would not usually find in decking. Because of the plastic in the material, it can raise the temperature of the deck quite a bit, so just be conscious of that. If you do not have an area shaded by a wall or trees, consider going for a lighter color so that it does not retain as much of the heat, otherwise you might burn your feet on really sunny days.

Composite decking is also easier to install the panels generally they have grooves on the underside that connect them. This also makes it easier to reuse. If you decide you want to move your deck or renovate your outdoor area, removing the composite decking and either placing it in storage or moving it to another area is not a big job. Moving traditional wooden decking may cause damage to the wood and you may end up having to purchase new planks. This is completely avoidable with composite decking!

Chapter 3:
Solar Panels - Time to Make the Call!

We have briefly mentioned solar power and why it's such a good option, but we are going to go a little more in-depth now. There are constantly new advances in this area, which is really exciting. We can expect new innovations in the next few years, which will push solar power to the next level.

Where Does Your Power Come From?

In general, America has made moves to improve energy production, and natural gases have overtaken coal as the primary source of power. Renewable energy sources have also been gaining popularity, this is excellent news, but every state is different.

It is essential to know where your utility company gets your electricity. If you live in a state that relies heavily on unsustainable methods of creating electricity, you should try and mitigate your own energy usage or change your source of energy. If you live in a state that uses cleaner ways of producing energy, you may not have to make drastic changes.

Since it is helpful to know where your state's energy is coming from. I have listed them in alphabetical order. Take a look and see the sources for power in your state. (This information was provided by Popovich (2018), and will change over time.)

• Alabama - Most of the energy is produced by natural gas (38%) with nuclear power and coal following behind with 30% and 22%, respectively.

• Alaska - Natural gas has consistently been the highest source of electricity for Alaska, providing

50% of the state's energy. Hydroelectric sources come in at 25%.

- Arizona - Nuclear power, coal, and natural gas provide 30%, 29%, and 27% of energy, respectively.

- Arkansas - Uses coal for 43% of its energy production, with natural gas providing 28%.

- California - 41% of California's power is produced by natural gases, with the remaining energy production obtained through various sources of renewable energy. This is great, but the state did purchase ¼ of its electricity from other states in 2017 when this study was completed, and those states use coal to produce energy.

- Colorado - Coal is used for 54% of energy production, with natural gases coming in second (23%).

- Connecticut - Nuclear (47%) and natural gas (46%) power are the top two energy producers in this state.

- Delaware - There was a massive shift from coal to natural gases in 2010. Now natural gases provide 89% of the energy in Delaware.

- Florida - Natural gases provide 67% of the energy, with coal at 16%.

- Georgia - Natural gas (41%), nuclear power (26%), and coal (25%) are the top energy producers.

- Hawaii - Petroleum is the main energy producer at 62%. We do see the state making plans to increase renewable energy sources, with solar power becoming more popular.

- Idaho - This state uses a majority of renewable energy sources, 61% is produced by hydroelectric sources. Wind power has also picked up.

- Illinois - 53% of power is generated from nuclear sources, and coal provides for 32% of the power.

- Indiana - Coal is still the number one producer of electricity, with 73%. Other energy sources are slowly creeping in, like natural gases and wind power.

- Iowa - Coal is still the number one energy producer sitting at 44%, but wind power has really taken off and comes in second at 37%.

- Kansas - Coal (38%) still provides the most energy, but wind energy (37%) is a close second.

- Kentucky - This state also relies heavily on coal (79%).

- Louisiana - Natural gases (60%) are number one, following far behind is nuclear power (16%).

- Maine - This state produces a lot of its energy from renewable sources, hydroelectric (30%), biomass (24%), and wind power (21%). However, it does import a lot of its energy from Canada, which needs to be taken into consideration.

- Maryland - Nuclear energy provides 43%, and coal sits at 24%.

- Massachusetts - Natural gas accounts for 66% of the power production, with nuclear power at 15%.

- Michigan - Coal produces 37% of the power, and nuclear comes in at 29%.

- Minnesota - Coal is still at the top with 39% but has declined to make room for nuclear (24%) and wind (19%) energy.

- Mississippi - Natural gases produce 77% of the energy, kicking coal off the top spot.

- Missouri - This state hasn't really made any changes in energy production as of yet. 80% of energy is produced by coal.

- Montana - Hydropower has increased in this state to 39%, coal is still number one at 49%.

- Nebraska - 60% of energy is produced by coal; however, we have seen a slight increase in nuclear and wind power in this state.

• Nevada - Natural gas overtook coal as the main energy source in 2005. It sits at 69% with solar power at second with 12%.

• New Hampshire - 57% of the energy is provided by nuclear power, and natural gases provide 20% of the energy in this state.

• New Jersey - Natural gases (49%) and nuclear (44%) are at the top.

• New Mexico - Collectively, natural gas and wind energy account for about half of the energy production in this state, coal is still number one at 54%.

• New York - 37% of energy is produced by natural gases and nuclear and hydroelectric sources following close behind.

• North Carolina - Nuclear is 33%, natural gases at 30%. Coal lagging behind at 27%.

• North Dakota - Coal is still number one at 64%, but wind energy (27%) is gaining on it.

• Ohio - Coal (57%) is slowly making way for natural gases and nuclear power.

• Oklahoma - Natural gases take the top spot with 41%, and wind energy (32%) is following closely behind.

- Oregon - Hydroelectric energy has always been popular here; it provides 61% of the energy in Oregon.

- Pennsylvania - Nuclear (39%), natural gases (34%), and coal (22%) are all pretty close. However, there has been a large decline in coal use.

- Rhode Island - Natural gases produce 94% of the electricity in this state; however, it also gets power from neighboring states.

- South Carolina - Nuclear (58%) and coal (19%) have been pretty consistent in this state.

- South Dakota - Hydroelectric sources and coal have been up and down for a while, but currently, most of the power is produced by hydroelectric sources with 48%. Wind power comes in at 27%.

- Tennessee - Nuclear power (40%) has overtaken coal (35%) as the number one power supplier.

- Texas - Natural gases (45%) and coal (30%) are the top two energy producers.

- Utah - Coal (70%) is still the number one producer of electricity, but it has declined slightly to make way for natural gases (16%). Solar power (7%) has also increased.

- Vermont - Almost all of Vermont's energy production is achieved through various renewable energy sources, hydroelectricity (57%) being number one. However, it does also purchase electricity from other states and Canada.

- Virginia - Natural gases are on top with 49%, and nuclear power follows behind it with 34%.

- Washington - Hydropower (71%) has been the number one source of energy production. The state also exports its electricity to other states and Canada.

- West Virginia - Coal is still the most used source of energy production, coming in at 93%. Considering that in 2001 it was 98%, we can see that West Virginia has barely made any progress in moving to cleaner and more renewable energy sources. This state does provide energy for multiple other states as well.

- Wisconsin - Coal is still the number one energy producer at 55%, nuclear power and natural gas follow behind.

- Wyoming - 86% of the power generated here is produced by coal. Wind power production has been slowly increasing; it currently sits at 9%. This state produces much more power than it can use, so it exports about 60% of it to other states.

It is worth noting that many of these states have plans in place to increase the amount of energy being produced by renewable energy sources. There is definitely improvement happening, which is great news. However, until these changes take place, it is each individual's responsibility to make sure they know where their energy is coming from and try to lessen their non-renewable power consumption. If you want to know in more detail how the states stack up against each other, have a look at <u>How does your state generates electricity?</u> You could also check out <u>Power Profile</u> to get a visual representation of the power generation in each state.

New Advances in 2020

While we can see that there has been a move towards greener energy sources, we need more of these sustainable sources so that we can cater for ourselves and the planet in the long term. Science and green technology is what will help us make this shift. We need more than just regular panels on roofs to pioneer this change. Let's take a look at the new innovations that we can expect to see in the near future.

500 W, 50-cell PV modules

This module was recently released by Risen Energy and Trina Solar, and it aims to bring down the cost per watt of installation labor. It will deliver about 31% more energy than the average panel, with the output of this module being about 380 W (Sylvia, 2020). These modules can be used on rooftops, where there is a limited amount of space; businesses and industries will be the ones to benefit the most from this technology. The goal is to eventually leverage the technology in this module on the lower output modules so that it can be available to residential users.

Floating Solar Farms

This technology is photovoltaic panels placed on the water surface, usually in reservoirs and dams. Placing these panels on the water means that there is less real estate being taken up for energy plants. These panels generate huge amounts of energy while having little to no impact on the environment. They also help with water management by preventing certain types of algae growing on the water's surface, and less evaporation has been seen since the panels absorb a large amount of the sunlight.

BIPV Solar Technology

BIPV stands for building-integrated photovoltaics. These panels actually blend into the architecture of buildings and homes: this means that instead of bringing down the aesthetic value of a building, they can add to it, or simply not be noticeable. As a homeowner, you will be able to save money on building materials and power costs when you use this kind of panels. They can be used as a building's facades, atriums, terraces floors, and canopies (Sandhu, 2019).

Solar Skins

These skins look similar to the regular solar panels, but there is a big difference here. Instead of being bright blue like regular solar panels, they display a custom picture to blend into the surface they are placed on. This technology takes the sunlight and allows it to filter through the skins into the cells underneath them. You could place these skins on your lawn or your roof to match their surfaces. Businesses can also benefit from this kind of panel if they choose to display logos or advertisements on them. These panels are a bit more expensive than traditional panels, which is to be expected.

If you are interested in this type of product, you can easily get a quote from Sistine's SolarSkins: Homeowners Quote. This quote will be brand specific, but you will still be able to get a good idea of the price range you may be looking at if you take the plunge. Feel free to do some research on other brands and see what fits you best. This type of technology is becoming more and more popular, so I'm sure you will have a few options to choose from.

Solar Fabric

This one is a real innovation! The reasoning behind it is that we experience solar radiation wherever we go so, why not have something to harness it? Pvilion and Tommy Hilfiger collaborated to design solar clothing, which captures the solar energy as you are out and about, then save it in a battery pack for later use.

This same technology is being used all over on carports, curtains, building awnings, and almost anything else you can think of. Creating technology that is both functional and usable is the goal, so even if you do not want to wear solar clothing, the technology can still be used in various other ways. Take a look at all the ways Pvilion have used their solar fabric at <u>Pvilion Projects</u>.

Photovoltaic Solar Noise Barriers

There has always been a high amount of noise caused by traffic in the US; that is why most states have built traffic noise barriers. The <u>US Department of Energy</u> has made a move to also use these traffic barriers for the generation of solar power. This means that there will be no additional space taken up for the generation of solar power.

Solar Power for Your Home

Now that you know more about solar energy production and the innovations that are being developed, you may want to dive into the world of solar power for yourself. The benefits of solar power are great, and it does actually save you money in the long run. I'm not going to lie to you, depending on where you live and how much energy you use, it can be pricey to install solar panels in your home, but it is an investment that is worth it.

If you would like to know how much solar panels may cost for you, this is a great tool to help you: Solar panel cost 2020: by state, by system size and by panel manufacturer. All you have to do is plug in your zip code to get started. This way, you can have a rough estimate of what it would cost you before you move forward with the process.

At a minimum, you would be looking at $11,004 for a 4kW system, going all the way up to $41,382 for a 20kW system. These prices are after-tax. There are various factors that play a part in determining the price of a solar system in your house, like the size of your house, where it is situated, what city or state you live in, how much electricity you use, and the type of solar panels you are looking to buy. It is always best to get a quote from a professional because what worked for a friend's house might not work for you.

The above website will also allow you to calculate how much you will be saving over a 25 year period: this is valuable information that will help you make an informed decision. The amount of money you can save will also vary depending on various factors, but to give you a rough estimate, you could be saving between $60,000 to $150,000 over your lifetime. So if you look at it realistically and in a worst-case scenario of needing the most expensive solar panel option with the lowest amount of savings, you will still come out with over $10,000 in savings in the long term. You could probably save a lot more than that, but the point is that solar energy will save you money in the long run even if you need the most expensive option.

Chapter 4:
Setting Up a Small Business

Starting a small business is an exciting endeavor to venture out into. There are so many benefits and rewards that come with it, and it is easy to see why there are 28 million small businesses in the US alone (Gregory, 2019). These form an integral part of the economy and the communities in which these businesses exist.

Starting up the business might just be the trickiest part. You need to have the right foundation in order for anything to succeed, so the planning and preparation before starting the business is actually the most important part. You need to know what you are doing and why you are doing it to make a success of it.

The Home Business

Starting a home business can be very rewarding and very enjoyable. Of course, there will be hard work involved in the process, but hard work is always easier when you enjoy what you do and are passionate about the end product you are delivering. Let's take a look at the why, in terms of starting your own business, before we dive into the how.

More Time

Time is a resource we all wish we had more of. The benefit of running your own business is that you have more control over your time. Yes, time will be needed to build up your business, but you will be in charge of your schedule. If you want to spend time with your family or have any kind of obligation during the day, you can go ahead and do it because you know that you can do the work late into the night if you have to. The restraint of a 9 to 5 is lifted, so you have more space to design the life you want to live because you have more pockets of time available for you to fill.

You will be able to go after your personal passions and pursuits. The business can be something that you really love, or it could be a way to finance what you love whilst giving you the time you need to pursue that thing. Of course, with all this flexible time, you will need to learn to manage it properly. You still need to work, so being disciplined with that is key.

Tax Benefits

Businesses get many more tax benefits than regular employees. When you run a home business, you can get tax benefits for your business and for yourself. You could potentially be able to write off internet and phone fees, supplies, utilities, and depending on the specific business and your situation. You might even be able to write off a portion of your car or home payments.

A home business will allow you to pay taxes on your net income, so that means that you can deduct all your expenses first and then pay taxes on what is left. This can significantly reduce the amount of taxes you pay. You should definitely make sure that you are following all applicable tax laws, so it's best to get a tax practitioner to guide you.

Be Your Own Boss

When you run your own business, you are your own boss. I think most people have had at least one job with a boss they cannot stand. Most of these tough bosses come across as being very forceful and harsh, but this is because they believe their way is right for the company. As frustrating as that is for you, they have the right to want the best for the company they care about.

When you work for yourself, you have that same power. You dictate how things are going to run. You make the rules. You decide how late you want to work when you want to work, what to wear to work, and there will be no one to micromanage you. If you are a person who values flexibility and freedom, this is the way to go.

Growth

Working a regular 9 to 5 job can sometimes leave you feeling stuck. Either there is no place to grow in the company, or it just feels like you are doing the same thing and following the same routine every single day. This is one of the top reasons people often aren't happy with their job.

That is something that you have the power to change when you run your own home business. If you feel stuck, you can change up your schedule, pick a different place to work, or work at a different time in the day. A small change like that can really help your productivity, and it is not a luxury usually available in a corporate job. In addition, the opportunities for financial and business growth rely on you and not someone else. You have the opportunity to learn more and grow more, both personally and for your business.

10 Steps for Setting Up a Small Business

Now that we have taken a look at everything, a home or small business can offer, we need to know the next steps in the process. Luckily there have been many that have gone before you, and we can learn from the experiences of others.

1. Research Is Key

If you have already determined what your product will be, whether a service or a physical product, you have to do research surrounding your business idea. In most cases, your product will already have an existing market. Do research on that market, see what it's like out there, and scope out the competition. If you can find out why other businesses in your niche are doing well, you will have the upper hand when you launch your business.

Spend time researching your target audience as well. You need to know who you are selling to and why they would buy your product. You would also like to know how to reach them and what attracts them to your product. The customers will be key to your business succeeding, so spend some time figuring out what they like. You could do focus groups or questionnaires to help with this process, but even just speaking to people will help you get the information you need.

2. Plan It Out

Most ideas and endeavors fail due to a lack of planning. Impulsive decisions and ill-informed moves can be the downfall of small businesses, so take time in the beginning to make a plan. You can change things up a bit as you move forward, gain experience, and obtain more knowledge, but you need a blueprint to start out with. Otherwise, you won't know which way you are going.

If you are planning on getting investors involved, you will need a very detailed business plan that they can look at to see where you are heading. A proper business plan is vital if you are trying to get others on board with you. Think about the steps you are going to take and how you are going to get buy-in from customers. Decide what resources you need to make your business a success. If you have everything written down, you will be more likely to take the steps you need to in order to make the business a success.

3. Plan Out Your Finances

When starting a small business, you will need to make some sort of financial investment. It doesn't have to cost you an arm and a leg, but some finances will definitely be involved. A simple way to draw up a financial plan is to think about what you will need to run this business for a year. These will include resources for your product, licenses, advertising, travel expenses, manufacturing, rent, and utilities. Every business is different, so you might need different things than what was mentioned, but whatever it is, make a comprehensive list.

Once you have your list of expenses, you need to develop a plan on how you are going to pay for what you need. Maybe you are going to finance your business entirely by yourself, or perhaps you want to get other people involved. A short term loan might also be an option worth looking at. Regardless, you will need a plan to ensure you will have the capital needed to get the business up and running.

4. Your Business Structure

The way in which you choose to structure your business influences quite a few factors, for example, your taxes and your business name. It would be worth it to do some research on the different business structures so you can make an informed decision. If your business is going to be complex, you might consider getting an attorney to help you make the right choice: they will be able to take you through the pros and cons of each structure. Some of the business structures you could choose from are an LLC, sole proprietorship, partnership, or corporation.

If you have chosen to go the LLC route, you can quite easily set your business up yourself. The best part is it is free, besides a small state fee in certain states. It is so quick and easy, I have done it as well. All you have to do is visit <u>LLC Filing & Business Formation - Start Your Company Today</u>, and follow the instructions.

5. Choose Your Name and Register It

The name of your business is very important: it is what people will know you by and recognize you as. You want the association to your business and your name to stick in your customers' minds and send across a good message. Take some time to think about the name you want to give your business; once it is up and running, it might be hard to change the name since people will already have an association with it.

Once you have your name, it is time to register your business. The process will vary depending on what your business structure is. If you have a sole proprietorship, you will have to register the name with your state clerk. Most of the other business structures will require you to complete and file the formation paperwork before you can register your business.

Make sure to check that no one else is using the name you chose for your business, and check if it is trademarked. While you are at it, check for and register your domain name: it is important to have an online presence so get to it as soon as possible. If the domain name you desire is not available, try using a catchphrase or something else that speaks to your company name and branding. You want everything to relate and be coherent.

6. Permits and Licenses

Some businesses need certain permits and licenses: this all depends on your product, size of your business, and your business structure. Different states have different requirements, so be sure to do research on what your state needs from you. Try and get to the paperwork as soon as possible as it may take a while before everything is sorted, and you do not want that to hold you back.

7. Get an Accounting System

You will need systems and processes in place for your business to run smoothly. One of the most important systems you need is an accounting system, as you need to be able to keep track of your money and assets. Your accounting system will manage your budget, spend, filing of taxes, and set the prices and rates of your product or service. This is all integral to the running of your business.

It is up to you whether you want to hire an accountant or handle the accounts on your own. If you opt to do it by yourself, you will need to choose the accounting software that works for you. There are plenty of options out there, but sit down and take a look at what you need and try and match that to the software you will be using. There is no use in paying for features you will never use.

8. Location

Location is an important aspect of a small business. Even if you are planning on running your business from home, you need to have a designated space for it. Think about what your business entails and the amount of space you need for it. Every business will need a different type of space and set up.

If you want to rent a place separate from your house, think about the area you want to rent in. Travel time to the office should be taken into consideration as well as the surrounding areas. If you need other vendors to purchase resources from, see if you can find somewhere close to the suppliers you need. On the other hand, if you want customers to visit your space to get the products, your business space needs to be somewhere that is easily accessible and seen.

Using a space in your home will have different requirements, but it is important to have a designated workspace. If you have a room or outbuilding that is separate from the house, this could be ideal for setting up a shop. Think about what you would need in terms of overall setup and work from there. At the end of the day, whether you choose a home office or to rent a space, it needs to be somewhere that is functional and comfortable.

9. Gather Your People

Regardless of the business model or the size of your business, you will need people around you. You may be thinking of hiring employees; in this case, sit down and think about the positions you need to fill. At the start of a business, you probably don't want to hire too many people: think about what positions could be merged and how you can work around that. Pick people you know will be there for you and can do the work. If you choose not to hire employees but rather want to outsource the work, you need to make sure you have a lawyer in place to help with contracts. Do research on the people you are outsourcing work to, as you want to make sure you are not overpaying and that they are capable of completing the work you have for them.

You may be wanting to go at this business solo, and that is perfectly fine, but it does not exempt you from the fact that you need people around you. You may not have employees or colleagues around you, but you still need people to support you and give you advice. The road to a small business can be a bumpy one, so make sure your people are there to help you and keep you motivated. Consider getting a coach or mentor who has been through the journey before. This person will be able to give you much-needed input: a mentor is valuable no matter what your business entails.

10. Get the Word Out There

There is no use of having your own business if no one knows you exist. You need a plan to start attracting customers and clients. Once your business is all step up and ready to go, this is the next important step. Look into advertising platforms and see how much they cost. Make use of your network: you will be surprised how much business you can get through word of mouth.

There are plenty of ways to get the word out there, you may have to pay for a marketing service to boost yourself at the beginning. Make sure you have a social media presence and have your website set up. The first place people go if they want to find something nowadays is the internet, so use it as a free advertising tool. An online presence also helps you connect with your consumers and get a feel for what they want.

Get yourself a mission statement and write a selling proposition. The mission statement is a short statement that will allow people to see what your business is and what it stands for. Everything you put out into the world should aim to draw people in. All your marketing will be tied to your brand. When working on your unique selling proposition, make sure you highlight what makes you different from the others in the market. Marketing is all about standing out so you can pull people in. Once you have a good following, it will be easier to grow your business.

Chapter 5:
Green Gardening

Having your own garden has many benefits: you know where your produce is coming from, it is better for the environment. Meals can very much leave you with a sense of satisfaction, knowing what you are eating is something you grew in a healthy garden yourself. Besides these benefits, just the fact that it gets you outside and allows you time for your mind to unwind and wander is beneficial to both your mental and physical health.

There are quite a few things you need to consider when you decide to garden and grow your produce. What you are capable of doing will be dependent on your goals and the space you have available. Luckily, there are many options to choose from, both in the kinds of plants you can grow and how you can grow them.

Organic vs. Standard Plants

Before we move on to growing a garden, it is important to understand the differences between organically grown plants and standard plant growing practices. Recently there has been more

63

of a shift towards organic gardening, however using pesticides and various fertilizers, often of unknown origin, is still the most popular method. Just because a way is most prominent or perhaps more convenient, it does not mean that it is the right way to go.

The standard way includes lots of synthetic pesticides, herbicides, and fertilizers: these are damaging not only to the environment but also to the health of the people who consume the plants. The reason that these products are popular is that they do help the plants grow quicker and bigger. They can help protect the plants from insects and also stop weeds from growing around the crops. Foods grown this way tend to have a lower amount of antioxidants, and these practices negatively impact the environment. These methods can hurt the environment by exposing the soil and water to substances that can cause soil degradation, and groundwater pollution.

For food or plants to be labeled organic, they need to have been grown using 95% organic material. There are quite strict standards when it comes to this: for example, there is usually a yearly inspection done on your farm if you claim to be an organic farmer. When you grow organically, you work in harmony with the environment instead of manipulating it. In the end, this is better for plants, animals, and the environment in general. When you choose to buy organically grown food, you are also supporting local farmers and small vegetable growers. That can help build a strong small economy and provides income for the people in your local community.

The Reason for Growing Your Own Garden

There are plenty of reasons people start growing their food and why you should also consider doing it. Gardening provides you with not only food but also the experience and accomplishment of growing something that you get to enjoy. Just this mere fact will make the food you grow yourself taste so much better than anything you can buy from the store.

Growing your produce allows you the opportunity to learn something new and keep learning. You will open up your mind to things that you have never thought of before. If you get your family involved, this can also be a great family activity: you will all be doing something together, getting your hands dirty, and getting some physical activity in. Last but not least, it can be a great way to save money. Most people do not know how much money they spend on fruit and vegetables regularly. If we are honest, there are plenty of times food in our refrigerators "turned" before we had the chance to use it.

Perhaps you are thinking of selling your produce: this is a great way to make money in a fulfilling and personal way. Selling your produce to local grocers or selling yourself at the local farmers' markets can put a few extra dollars in your pocket. You will have to deal with the initial investment and some maintenance, but the returns will be greater than the investment. I love the fact that you can freeze or dry out certain fruit, vegetables, and herbs to sell at a later stage. Pickling can also be a great way of preserving your produce to sell it throughout the year. Many people are interested in buying organically grown produce, so once you get the word out there, you'll find that people are willing to purchase from you.

What to Grow

There are many different plants that you could grow in your garden, but as a beginner gardener, the best kind of plants will be those that give you a high yield and do not cost much. These plants also have a higher tolerance to pests than most others, making them easier to care for. We are going to chat about a few options you have for a low maintenance and high-yield garden.

Leafy greens are a great way to go because they grow in abundance and survive slightly cooler weather. Lettuce is the best choice out of the leafy greens: the yield is high, and the plants tend to be quite healthy. Bonus, you can pick off the leaves you need, and after just one week, more leaves will have grown to replace them!

Tomatoes are well worth planting as well: not only do they have a high yield, but you will get so much use out of them since they are in so many dishes and sauces. The harvesting season for most tomatoes is quite long, so you will have plenty even as the weather starts cooling down. Just think about all the things you add tomatoes to, and you will agree that they are well worth planting and harvesting.

All types of squash, be it zucchini, winter, yellow squash, are high-yielding plants. You do have to make sure you have the space for them as these are quite big plants that produce a lot. If you do not have space, it is best to go for zucchini and plant them in a box: they do quite well in an enclosed environment. Squash also freezes well, so you do not have to use it all from fresh.

Green beans are another high-yielding plant. There is nothing like eating fresh green beans, but they absolutely taste great after being frozen.

Pole beans will produce more than most bush beans, producing extra veggies for a long season.

Who doesn't love cucumbers? They are great eaten fresh in a salad and awesome when they are pickled and added to food. It's a good thing that they are also on the list of high-yield plants. You may have to give some away to friends and family or sell some since you will be getting quite an abundance from these plants, and cucumbers do not freeze well.

Chili peppers or hot peppers are also a good choice. They can survive in both hot and cooler climates, plus they do not need much attention. As long as you remember to water them, you should be good. People often pick them when they are green since they are hotter at that time. You can wait a while or pick them and let them ripen off the plant.

There has been some debate about whether rhubarb is a fruit or vegetable. However, where most can agree is that it is a great garden plant. Rhubarb can pretty much be left to its own devices and give you a really good amount of produce when spring comes around.

Let's move on over and talk about some fruit that is awesome to plant in your garden! Blueberry bushes are both beautiful to look at and can yield a good amount of berries in season. If you do not have lots of space or just prefer not to have huge plants in your garden, opt for the dwarf bushes, which only grow to about two to four feet high. If anything, planting blueberry bushes will save you money since these little berries can be quite expensive, whether they are in season or not.

The final plant I want to mention that is both high-yielding and low maintenance is the blackberry bush. Boys (2017) suggest growing Triple Crown Thornless Blackberries because they give off a lot of fruit during harvest, and the flavor is exceptional. As with blueberries, these can be quite expensive to buy from a store, so growing them at home is a much cheaper option. You can always freeze any leftovers to use in cooking and baking dishes later on in the year when they are no longer in season.

Howard (2018) agrees with the most of the plants that have been mentioned by saying that the plants that will offer the best yield in a short time frame with a limited amount of space are indeterminate tomatoes, pole beans, zucchini, swiss chard, tall snow peas, and sugar snaps. These plants generally keep producing until the weather gets frosty. You just need to make sure you keep picking and trimming them. They are low maintenance if you do pay attention to them when needed.

That just shows you that there are so many different plants to try out and grow when you are a beginner, have limited space, or just want a low maintenance garden. Of course, if you have the time, space, and resources to grow other vegetables that require a bit more from you, go for it. Either way, gardening is rewarding, and you might find that you are a lot more motivated to take care of your plants if they will give you produce that you enjoy eating. So take a few moments to think about what you want your garden to look like and what kind of fruits and veggies you truly enjoy eating. Once you have done that and are happy with the plants you have chosen, you are ready to start!

Herbs

I didn't talk about herbs in the previous section because I wanted to mention them separately. Herbs can provide you with a lucrative income if you wish to sell them, but there are also many other benefits to growing them, so let's take some time to chat about herbs and which ones you should be growing.

Herbs are some of the best low maintenance plants out there. They do not need a lot of attention, are pretty resilient to pests, and don't need extremely high-quality soil to thrive. You will be able to keep your herbs for a very long time and dry them out to use later, as they will retain their fragrance and flavor. As you know, herbs are in nearly every recipe, so planting them is well worth the initial investment.

Some herbs are just better to plant than others. That is because these herbs are both profitable if you wish to sell them and easy to grow. The best herbs to grow for culinary purposes are basil, chives, cilantro, oregano, and parsley. You will find these herbs in almost every kitchen, whether in dried, powdered, or whole form: this just shows you how in demand they are. If you take a look in your cupboard, you are likely to find these herbs somewhere.

Now some herbs are not used for culinary purposes, but some have medicinal value or another use. These herbs are also popular, and you should consider growing these for yourself and enough to sell to others. These are catnip, chamomile, lavender, marshmallow, and St John's wort. These herbs are very popular, and each of them provides specific benefits: look into growing a few to reap the medicinal benefits from them.

If you are thinking of selling herbs for an income, you may want to think about growing herbs that are not very common. Chefs and foodies are always on the lookout for something unique to add to their dishes' flavor profiles. In the spring and summer months, you could even sell potted herbs so that your customers can grow the plants themselves. In cooler months, you can switch to selling dried varieties, herbal teas, and natural remedies. Herbs can provide you with income all year round if you plan for the cooler months.

Getting Started

So you want to have an organic garden, but don't know where to start? Then you have come to the right place. As we have discussed, growing your own garden has many benefits. Going through this process will leave you with a feeling of accomplishment, and you will get some delicious fresh vegetables out of it.

The Right Tools

Like with anything you start, you will need the right tools for the job. Gardening is more than just placing a seed in the ground and hoping you get a plant next spring. The right tools will set you up for success and will make gardening easier and more enjoyable. All of the products mentioned can be purchased from your local garden supply store or even on Amazon.

You will need clippers, a trowel set, a soil test kit, a compost bin, gardening gloves, and a watering can. You could also speak to a specialist who can help you decide on other tools to help your specific situation. They can also tell you where it would be best to place your garden and give you a whole host of other useful information.

The Soil

People need nutrients to be healthy and grow: the same is true of plants. The difference between us is that plants get their nutrients from the soil, so we need to make sure the soil we plant in is of good quality and has high nutrient value.

If you want to test your soil quality, there are two ways you can go. The first way is to buy a soil testing kit: you will place your sample in there, and it will give you a breakdown of what is in the soil. The second way is to send a sample of your soil to your local agricultural extension office. There will be a small fee to pay, but you will get a complete breakdown of the soil nutrients and the pH balance. They will also be able to give you recommendations on how to treat the soil and advise you on the way forward.

The best time to test your soil is in the fall. The reason for this is that if you have to apply any organic nutrients to your soil, you can do this in winter to make sure your soil will be ready in spring. You will want to add manure and make sure that you have added some compost: these will give the soil the nutrients it needs to grow healthy plants. Manure comes from livestock, so when you go out to get your supplies, make sure you choose a manure that has come from organically and sustainably raised livestock. Your manure should be composted with other materials unless you plan to add it to your garden a few months later. Once you have added these to the soil, it will be in good condition to start working for you!

Composting

I mentioned above that you should be adding compost to your soil. The best thing you can do is make the compost yourself. Compost can include nearly any organic material that you have in your house: this is a great way to reduce your household waste, and it provides the plants with lots of nutrients they need to grow strong.

The best compost has the right balance of carbon and nitrogen. If you have the means to test your compost, you can do that, but the exact chemistry is not usually too important. You will still be able to get great results by keeping it simple. Carbon-rich material will be leaves, sawdust, and any trimmings you get from your garden. Nitrogen-rich material will be kitchen scraps, old vegetables, etc.

First, layer the carbon-rich material, then place a thin layer of soil on top and follow that with a nitrogen-rich material layer. You can continue layering until you have run out of material and then top the whole thing with about five inches of soil.

As you add in new layers, the compost will need to be turned and moistened. You can do this by adding some water to the pile: you don't have to soak it, but slightly moist is good. The pile should not smell, but if you are getting a stretch from it, it is an indication that you should be adding more carbon material. Add it in and give it a turn, and your pile should be less smelly. The compost should be ready to use in about two months, depending on the weather as it does take a bit longer if the weather is colder. Once your material has finished composting, you can add it to your soil.

Choosing Your Plants

When it comes to picking some great plants to grow, it pays to do a bit of research for your area. Some plants will grow better in certain environments than others, so knowing what fits your location is key to a happy and healthy garden. Even on your property, there will be smaller microenvironments that will suit certain plants more than others. You will have to be aware of the light, moisture, drainage, and quality of the soil (Howard, 2018).

If you are looking for plants that are best suited for your local climate and area, the best place to go is your local farmers market, where people will sell plants, seeds, and seedlings that will most likely survive the local conditions. The vendors will also be able to give you advice on how and where to grow the specific plants, so pay attention to what they tell you and ask lots of questions. If you plan on buying seedlings, opt for younger ones, and do not have many blooms: this generally means that they do not have overcrowded root systems and will be easier to transplant to your garden.

Get Planting

There is no gardening without planting, and it isn't just about digging a hole and putting the seed or seedling in. It requires a little more strategy than that! Again, you will have to think about the space you have and the best way to use it.

Grouping your plants properly is the best way to go. Grouping allows all the same plants to be together, making it easier to water and place compost. It can also reduce the amount of time you will spend weeding, and we all like that idea! "I love weeding!" said no one, ever. Creating raised beds in rows is a good idea because it will create space for you to walk and create space between plants.

Watering

Remember when we spoke about rainwater harvesting a little earlier on in the book? Here would be a great place to use that rainwater.

You do not have to water your plants every day: doing so would likely damage the plants and cause fungal growth. About an inch of water a week should be sufficient, and this includes water from rainfall, so if there was heavy rainfall in your area, there would be no need to water. When you infrequently water with extra time in between each session, it encourages the plant's roots to grow deeper into the ground to search for water. Deeper roots mean stronger plants!

When watering, try and concentrate the water at

the plant's base and not on the leaves or greenery. The tops of the plants are more prone to damage and disease. Try and not water your plants in the evening as the water will take a long time to soak up: this is a fungal risk. Watering as early as you can in the morning is the best option. That will give the plants enough time to soak up water, and because it is not as hot in the morning, it will lessen the amount of evaporation that takes place.

Get the Weeds Outta There

Weeds are an inevitable occurrence when it comes to gardening: it happens no matter where you live and what you do. Be prepared for this. You will have to do some weeding to make sure your garden stays healthy.

Weeds steal the nutrients that you have added for your plants, and they may suffocate them if left to their own devices. It is a good excuse to get outside, and pulling out weeds counts as exercise, so at least you get a bit of fresh air and physical activity out of it.

If you want to reduce the number of weeds that grow around your plants, you can add a mulch layer around the area. You can make your mulch from various things, including sawdust, wood chippings, garden materials, hay, or even just a burlap layer. If you opt for the higher nitrogen options, make sure your plants are those that need the higher nutrient content. Otherwise, this could negatively impact your plant growth.

Plant Protection

Since our aim here is to create an organic garden, we will not use pesticides to protect our plants. There are plenty of all-natural ways to protect our beloved garden, but you need to make sure that there isn't an underlying reason your garden has excessive pests. Diversity in the types of plants you have will mean that your garden will not get infested with a large amount of one type of pest. Also, check that your plants are getting enough water, sunlight, and nutrients. If your plants are healthy and strong, they will be a bit more resilient.

Creating a welcoming space for natural pest predators is one of the best forms of natural pest control. Frogs, lizards, and predatory insects will be your best friends when it comes to protecting your garden. Make sure there is a source of water nearby and try and grow a few plants that blossom, as this will attract the friendly predators. If you are not keen on this, you can opt for setting a net over your garden to keep pests out. There are some other options like chili pepper sprays, garlic, and certain organic oils and soaps.

Harvesting

After all that hard work, you will eventually reap the fruits (or veggies) of your labor. Harvesting is probably the most satisfying part of the whole process. The best tool to harvest your produce will be sharp scissors: avoid breaking off the plants with your hands since this can cause some unwanted damage. Check your garden daily or every other day when it is peak harvest season: you would be surprised at how fast some plants grow in optimal conditions.

If you have planted leafy greens like spinach or kale, don't pick them all from the same place. Rather pick them randomly to leave some on each plant. Don't worry if you think there is too much food as you can always sell it or freeze it for later.

After a Successful Growing Season

Now that you have your bounty of produce don't forget to clean up and maintain your garden. The preparation you do when your garden is not actively growing will determine whether you will have a successful crop next harvest season.

Do a thorough check of your garden and make sure there are no sick or diseased plants around. If there are, pull them out of the ground and make sure that there is nothing left over, even stray leaves can cause other plants to get sick, and you do not want that. You can get rid of any infected plants by burying them far away from your garden or preferably destroying them with fire. That is a perfect excuse for an outdoor bonfire.

You can keep the other healthy plants in the ground for now. It will help protect the soil from erosion, damage, and weeds. If you plan to get rid of some annual plants, chop them off instead of pulling them out of the ground. Too much pulling will result in damaged soil, and this way, you leave the roots in the ground.

Gardening Systems

Gardening systems are a worthwhile investment if you want to grow your plants for a longer period or even all year round. They are an investment, so be prepared to spend a bit of cash on them in the beginning. However, the return on investment is worth it since you will not have to worry about the seasonality of the plants you are growing: it is also quite interesting and rewarding to see your plants yielding produce throughout the year. There are three different gardening systems that we will be going through in this section.

Greenhouses

Greenhouses are a classic way to grow plants and keep them healthy. You have most likely heard or dreamt about having one in your yard at some point. The structure can be large or small, but you will need to carve out some space outside to set up a greenhouse. Most people usually end up wanting or needing a bit more space than they initially thought, so make sure that you are realistic and give yourself a bit of extra space just in case.

As you know, a greenhouse structure has a clear outer material that lets the sun in and then keeps the greenhouse heat from escaping quickly. That helps to create a warmer climate than most of us have naturally. The greenhouse may have with thermostats that automatically control the temperature with fans or open windows for a climate-controlled environment. At night or in colder temperatures, the greenhouse remains warm. This system provides the right environment for many plants to thrive, even plants that normally do not do well in winter.

As the greenhouse is an enclosed area, you will have much more control over what goes on inside. Your plants will not be subject to the elements outside, and only the rare pest will sneak in. You can usually assemble it yourself unless you think of getting a very large or elaborate greenhouse installed. In terms of the nutrients and care that the plants need in a greenhouse, it is the same as outdoor gardening because your plants will still get their nutrients from the soil. Bonus, you may not have to water them as much due to the greenhouse humidity!

Hydroponics

Hydroponics has gained major popularity in the gardening community in recent years. The big draw of this system is that you do not need to have a lot of space and can grow plants indoors or on a balcony: this provides people who live in small houses or apartments to grow their produce under restricted conditions. The plants grown in this system do not need soil to grow as they are given nutrients in a soluble form.

The initial purchase can be expensive, but there are many different options if you are interested in getting a hydroponic system. It will be a great investment, and the upkeep is relatively economical once everything is in place. Greenhouse Growing (2020) gives us the six main types of hydroponics systems: aeroponics, wick systems, drip systems, deep water culture (DWC), nutrient film technique (NFT), and the ebb and flow or flood and drain systems.

You will need to be aware of the fact that the plants grown in a hydroponic system will need to be cared for or checked up on daily. So if you are someone who does not have the time or is not keen on looking after something every day, this may not be the system for you unless you are willing to make a change to accommodate it.

This system does not use soil to remove any barriers the roots have to get to water and nutrients. That allows the plants to grow at a faster rate than the more traditional methods. Plants grown in hydroponic systems can grow about 20% faster and yield around 25% more produce than the same plants grown in the soil (Epic Gardening, 2019). However, to reap these benefits, you will need to take care of this system properly. Since it is not a natural system, you will be creating an artificial environment for your plants: that does mean you are in control of everything, so you will have to be willing to actively do that.

This system's other benefits include lack of pests and disease, lower water usage, no chemicals extra needed, and no limitations due to space or season. If you have the money to spend on the initial purchase, I believe it is worthwhile to get a hydroponics system.

Vertical and Wall Gardening

Vertical gardening is a great solution if you have limited space, which helps solve a few other problems. Since the plants are up off the ground, they receive better air circulation and reduces the risk of being destroyed by weeds and animals. You can choose to build a vertical garden hydroponically or by using more traditional soil methods. It's also a great option for older people and those with limited mobility as it allows them to still enjoy gardening with less physical labor and bending required.

You will not be giving up produce yield when you choose to take up vertical gardening. There are also quite a few options in terms of what you can use to build your vertical garden, and it can truly add to the aesthetic of your house if done correctly. You could use shelves, hanging baskets, and even trellises. When you choose the soil option, you will be able to design it how you want and can even use recycled materials to make the containers for your plants.

If you are planning on going the hydroponic route, you will have to purchase a vertical hydroponic system to facilitate your garden. There are quite a few options, and they come in a variety of price points. Amazon has quite a large selection of systems for you to choose from. If you are interested in looking at what Amazon has to offer, then take a look at the options available Vertical Hydroponic. There are also a number of other places you can get a hydroponic system from. Want to buy local? Go for it, and I love that as well! Check with your local nurseries and see if they have any available. The nursery personnel may well know of a great local supplier. The professionals working there will also guide you along the process and give you tips for your specific needs and area. Once you have decided which route you will be going, all that is left is to purchase your system and get planting.

Indigenous Yards

Perhaps you are not keen on growing your own produce, which is perfectly fine: there is still value in growing a great garden. You can have a beautiful garden that does not produce crops, but still provides many benefits for you and the environment. Having an indigenous yard is one way to go. An indigenous yard is a garden that focuses on planting plants that are indigenous to the area instead of just using plants commonly found in nurseries.

Currently, the trend is to have a perfectly grassed lawn with a fountain, statues, and maybe a flower patch or bush here and there. That may seem like the best way to go, but the truth is that urbanization has destroyed many plants' habitats. So the land on which you live probably has numerous alien species pushing out what was originally found on the land. That will affect the local birds and other animals that live in that area. Alien plants become a nuisance to indigenous species, which sadly hardly stand a chance against the alien species.

This is why it is important to consider growing a garden filled with indigenous plants, as it will foster the reparation of the natural environment and ecosystem. That can benefit you as well: you will be creating a beautiful garden that will attract many different kinds of birds, butterflies, and other interesting insects.

Once planted and given the right nutrients, these plants can survive on their own. This their "homeland," and they have adapted to live in it, so there will be a lot less work for you to help them thrive. Since they are much lower maintenance than other plants, you will also be saving water. These native plants will reward you by giving you beautiful foliage and flowers, and you will be able to enjoy the show as the seasons change. It can truly be a rewarding experience to see how just a small change can bring about something beautiful.

Chapter 6:
Selling Your Produce

Now that you have got your garden all set up and are growing beautiful produce, your next step might be to sell what you have grown. Your plants will often give you a bigger bounty than you know what to do with, which creates a great business opportunity for you. If you love gardening, this is a great way to get paid for something you love to do.

Overview of Requirements

You do not have to just sell your fresh fruit, vegetables, and herbs. You can use your yield to make products such as cookies, cakes, other baked goods, jams, and much more: the possibilities are truly endless, especially if you enjoy cooking and baking.

There are a few requirements that you will have to follow if you do decide to do this. Certain foods are prohibited from being sold, while others have stricter regulations for selling than others. You will need to be aware of these before you jump into your business venture. Each state has different requirements for different food items, and we will highlight that in the next section. For now, let's talk about the common requirements you will come across.

Labeling and Ingredients

In most cases, when you are selling from individual to individual, the rules are not too strict. You can sell most baked goods, dry baking mixes, jars of jams and jellies, and even some candies. The standard is that you should have everything labeled, as the customer has to know exactly what is in whatever they are buying.

The labels should state the ingredients in order of the highest volume or weight used. All ingredients should be listed: even if a minute amount was used, state the ingredient's volume or weight next to that ingredient. The label should also include the business name, your name and address, and state that the product has been homemade. The more information you have on the label, the better since it also helps the customer buy your product.

Permits and Licenses

Many states have rules in place that limit selling to restaurants, grocery stores, and other public consumer places. You can most likely start selling to individuals or at farmers' markets without a permit but will have to get a permit or license if you want to sell more commercially. Each state will have a different process, so make sure you do your research concerning this.

When you apply for your permit or license, there are a few standard things to expect. The competent authority will probably do a kitchen inspection to ensure you have the right equipment, clean space, and no animals and pets allowed in the area. Often they will require you to have a completely separate kitchen to your home kitchen. You will have to have proof of this and that the commercial kitchen will need to be inspected before issuing the license or permit.

You will also have to take into account that most states do not allow you to sell goods over state lines. You may have a website that promotes your business, and people may be able to order online: this is fine but make sure you make it clear that your products are only available in your state unless you have gotten a permit that allows you to sell across state lines.

Commercial Kitchen

Most of us do not have thousands of dollars available to build or buy a commercial kitchen for our business ventures. This can be a big block in your business dreams, but the good news is that there is another way. You can actually rent a commercial kitchen: these kitchens have already been inspected and are ready to use. All you have to do is book it for the time you need and then get cooking or baking.

If you plan out your cooking or baking in advance, you can rent it out a few times a month. This is really convenient, and it's an option available in many areas. Most commercial kitchens for rent are available at various price points, so you should be able to find something that will meet your needs.

If you are looking for a commercial kitchen to rent, take a look at these websites:

• The Kitchen Door: this website is easy to navigate, all you have to do is type in your zip code, and it will bring up all commercial kitchens for hire in your area. If you have a commercial kitchen space, you can also make it available to rent on the website and get business from it - The Kitchen Door: Find Commercial and Commissary Kitchen Rentals.

• Peerspace: Also, a very easy to navigate website that will provide you options on commercial kitchen spaces near you. These spaces are available to rent by the hour and vary from cafe kitchen to professional kitchens. You are bound to find something that suits your needs - Here's Where to Rent Commercial Kitchen Space by the Hour.

Requirements in Different states

Each state has different requirements about which types of food you can and cannot sell. Even within these regulations, there are other requirements regarding how the food is prepared and many other things. It is best to be aware of what your state requires from you so that you are not doing anything illegal or causing you problems in the future.

Below I have listed the states in alphabetical order, with a link leading to information regarding each state's requirements and regulations as provided by Pick Your Own (n.d.):

• Alabama - Alabama Cottage Food Laws and Regulations: How to sell your homemade foods in Alabama

• Alaska - Selling non-hazardous foods is permitted in Alaska when being sold directly to a customer (Pick Your Own, n.d.). You should contact your local environmental health officer to clarify if you are not sure of something. -

○ Cottage Food Fact Sheet athttp://www.pickyourown.org/cottagefood/Alaska-cottage-food-guide.pdf

○ Cottage Food Exemptions athttp://www.pickyourown.org/cottagefood/Alaska-cottage-food-exemptions.pdf

- Arizona - <u>Arizona Cottage Food Laws and Regulations: How to sell your homemade foods in Arizona</u>

- Arkansas - <u>Arkansas Cottage Food Laws and Regulations: How to sell your homemade foods in Arkansas</u>

- California - <u>California Cottage Food Laws and Regulations: How to sell your homemade foods in California</u>

- Connecticut - <u>Connecticut Cottage Food Laws and Regulations: How to sell your homemade foods in Connecticut</u>

- Colorado - <u>Colorado Cottage Food Laws and Regulations: How to sell your homemade foods in Colorado</u>

- Florida - <u>Florida Cottage Food Laws and Regulations: How to sell your homemade foods in Florida</u>

- Georgia - <u>Georgia Cottage Food Laws and Regulations: How to sell your homemade foods in Georgia</u>

- Hawaii - <u>Hawaii Cottage Food Laws and Regulations: How to sell your homemade foods in Hawaii</u>

- Idaho - This state has seven districts that act independently; each health district has different regulations. Please go to the Idaho Health and Welfare website and find your district to get accurate information - www.healthandwelfare.idaho.gov

• Illinois - Illinois Cottage Food Laws and Regulations: How to sell your homemade foods in Illinois

• Indiana - Indiana Cottage Food Laws and Regulations: How to sell your homemade foods in Indiana

• Iowa - Iowa Cottage Food Laws and Regulations: How to sell your homemade foods in Iowa

• Kentucky - Kentucky Cottage Food Laws and Regulations: How to sell your homemade foods in Kentucky

• Maine - Maine Cottage Food Laws and Regulations: How to sell your homemade foods in Maine

• Maryland - Maryland Cottage Food Laws and Regulations: How to sell your homemade foods in Maryland

• Massachusetts - Massachusetts Cottage Food Laws and Regulations: How to sell your homemade foods in Massachusetts

- Michigan - <u>Michigan Cottage Food Laws and Regulations: How to sell your homemade foods in Michigan</u>

- Mississippi - <u>Mississippi Cottage Food Laws and Regulations: How to sell your homemade foods in Mississippi</u>

- Missouri - <u>Missouri Cottage Food Laws and Regulations: How to sell your homemade foods in Missouri</u>

- Nebraska - <u>Nebraska Cottage Food Laws and Regulations: How to sell your homemade foods in Nebraska</u>

- New Hampshire - <u>New Hampshire Cottage Food Laws and Regulations: How to sell your homemade foods in New Hampshire</u>

- New Jersey - <u>New Jersey Cottage Food Laws and Regulations: How to sell your homemade foods in New Jersey</u>

- New Mexico - <u>Food Program</u>

- New York - <u>New York Cottage Food Laws and Regulations: How to sell your homemade foods in New York</u>

- North Carolina - <u>North Carolina Cottage Food Laws and Regulations: How to sell your homemade foods in North Carolina</u>

- Ohio - Ohio Cottage Food Laws and Regulations: How to sell your homemade foods in Ohio

- Oklahoma - Oklahoma Cottage Food Laws and Regulations: How to sell your homemade foods in Oklahoma

- Oregon - Oregon Cottage Food Laws and Regulations: How to sell your homemade foods in Oregon

- Pennsylvania - Pennsylvania Cottage Food (Limited Food Establishments) Laws and Regulations: How to sell your homemade foods in Pennsylvania

- South Carolina - South Carolina Cottage Food Laws and Regulations: How to sell your homemade foods in South Carolina

- South Dakota - South Dakota Cottage Food Laws and Regulations: How to sell your homemade foods in South Dakota

- Tennessee - Tennessee Cottage Food Laws and Regulations: How to sell your homemade foods in Tennessee

- Texas - Texas Cottage Food Laws and Regulations: How to sell your homemade foods in Texas

- Utah - <u>Utah Cottage Food Laws and Regulations: How to sell your homemade foods in Utah</u>

- Vermont - <u>Vermont Cottage Food Laws and Regulations: How to sell your homemade foods in Vermont</u>

- Virginia - <u>Virginia Cottage Food Laws and Regulations: How to sell your homemade foods in Virginia</u>

- Washington state - <u>Washington state Cottage Food Laws and Regulations: How to sell your homemade foods in Washington state</u>

- West Virginia - <u>West Virginia Cottage Food Laws and Regulations: How to sell your homemade foods in West Virginia</u>

- Wisconsin - <u>Wisconsin Cottage Food Laws and Regulations: How to sell your homemade foods in Wisconsin</u>

- Wyoming - <u>Wyoming Cottage Food Requirements</u>

Your Sales Strategy

So you've checked out the requirements and are happy with what you have, which means you are ready to sell. Before you go out into the market and start selling your wares, you should work on a strategy. If you have a game plan, it will give you a better chance of getting your products sold and getting a good price for them. You can sell privately and earn a good living out of it, but if you want to take things a step further, you can try your hand at selling to restaurants and grocery stores.

Selling to Restaurants

When you try and sell your gardens wonderful fruits and veggies to a restaurant, remember that they want the best for their business, as most restaurants are individually or family-owned. The great thing about selling to restaurants is that you can work together in deciding what to grow. If you have good, regular customers, you will be able to speak to the chef and see what kinds of fruit, vegetables, or other produce they need in different seasons. This way, you can grow specific kinds of plants, and nothing will go to waste.

You want to show them why your brand of produce is worth buying. Once you have one person say yes, you have a testimony to help you make the second and third sale, so focus on getting one, and the rest will be a little easier to convince. If you are really good and your product lives up to expectations, people will start coming to you instead of you having to go out to find someone to purchase from you. So let's focus on how you can get that first sale.

Research Your Audience

As with most things, research is needed to be successful in this endeavor. You will need to know which restaurants source their produce locally and which do not. If they do not buy locally, find out why and see if you can solve whatever is stopping them. It might be that local produce is too expensive for them, or maybe they are not aware of any local suppliers: these might be the kinds of problems you can solve.

If they do source locally, find out what they look for and anything they are missing that you can provide for them. Filling a need is one of the best ways to get someone to buy into what you are selling. Take a look at how they receive their products and how they go about buying them. If they go to farmers' markets and just buy what is available, you can plan with them to grow what they need and then deliver it to them. If you can make their lives easier, they will appreciate that and be more willing to listen to what you have to say.

Be Aware of Trends and Hard-to-Find Crops

When targeting restaurants, you should be aware of food trends and crops that are generally hard to come by. When chefs develop restaurant menus, they attract customers to get the food they don't get at home, so their needs will be different from a regular grocer. Chances are they will want organic berries, tomatoes, and corn rather than the much more common potatoes and onions (although I grow those too!)

Keep up to date with food trends by checking the internet and by following great food blogs and famous chefs when you come across them. They will usually set the tone for what most restaurants follow, and if you are ahead of the trends, you will be able to plan to grow certain produce in advance so that it is ready when the trend is in full swing. That will give you a head start and gain loyalty from customers.

Even just taking a chance and growing something that is not grown often could set you apart. The restaurant game is very competitive, so many restaurateurs are looking for an edge: if you can provide something quite different, you will want to show them that your products can give them that edge. That is a great way to break into the restaurant market. The plants don't even have to be the hardest to grow. Just keep an eye open on any possible competitors and try and set yourself apart!

Meet the Chefs and Owners

Relationships are always key to business and in life in general. If you want to be successful in this space, you will have to put yourself out there and meet the people who could be potential buyers. Going to the restaurants to approach them is one strategy you can employ, but there is something to be said about 'chance meetings.'

Try and visit local food events. Most cities usually have plenty to choose from, and you want to make yourself a regular in the local food community. If possible, find out which events the restaurant owners and chefs you are keen on working with are attending. You could even volunteer at these events, this will help you meet more people, and if you volunteer by offering your goods, you can get the word out about your high-quality edibles. The more you immerse yourself in the food community, the more likely you will meet people who can help you out, give you support, or even become potential new customers.

Plan in Advance

Remember that when you are just starting out, you probably can't deliver the moon, so be realistic. You will have to test out your capabilities and see what you are good at growing, so start small and work on a few types of plants well: good quality is much better than a large quantity of mediocre produce. The quality will help you retain the buyers you have. As you get more experienced, you can branch out and try different kinds of fruit and vegetables.

Meet with your customer at the beginning of the growing season to see their menu plan. This way, you will have a good idea of what they need, and you can work with them to provide them with the right choices. You should decide beforehand what you are capable of growing so that you can make the customer aware in advance: there is nothing worse than promising you can do something and not being able to deliver. Take along an organic seed catalog so they can see what is possible and what is not. If you are prepared before you get there, it will show that you know what you are talking about, which will increase your credibility.

Retain the Relationships

Changes will definitely happen in the restaurant industry, and your customers may want to change up their suppliers. You should make sure you are always in the loop about this, and the best way to do this is to maintain the relationships you have with the managers, chefs, or owners. If you keep the relationship alive, they will be more likely to tell you when things are changing. They need to remember you and have a feeling of loyalty towards you, and this can only be built through ongoing relationships.

Pop by the restaurant every once in a while just to find out if you can help, or even better, give them some of your best harvests to try out. Don't be overbearing, as you do want to foster genuine relationships with your clients. It won't only help the direct relationship, but people are more likely to recommend people who they like and have relationships with, so it may even result in new customers for you.

Hand Out Samples

Who doesn't like free samples? This is such a great way to get your products out there, as people are more likely to buy something they have already tried. When you go for meetings, take some of your goods with you, never go in empty-handed: remember your business is food, so provide that to them. If you already have existing customers, send them some free samples of other fruit and vegetables you have grown along with their regular order. Sometimes people need to experience something new before they know they need it. Even if they do not order it for the next time, they will appreciate the kind gesture, which will bolster your relationship.

Don't Exclude Smaller Restaurants

Small restaurants may not pay as much as larger, more established restaurants, but that does not mean that they won't provide you with good business. Smaller restaurants are usually more loyal than the bigger guys, and they are more likely to use word of mouth to find suppliers. This means that you could get more clients this way. You should aim to have many different customers because you don't know how long someone will want to use your products, and you don't want to be left without an income.

Deliver on Your Promises

I have mentioned this a few times in other points, but it is very important that you are the one who delivers on their promises. If you don't, you could end up creating a bad reputation for yourself. The restaurant community is small, and word gets around quickly, so if you have not lived up to expectations, it might not just stay between you and the customer.

Set realistic expectations and always grow extra just in case something goes wrong. Sometimes things happen that are out of your control, but you should do your best to plan for the unexpected: it is much better to have more than to have too little. When you are starting out, be honest about what you can deliver and grow from there. Being consistent and reliable will do much more for your business than anything else.

Selling to Grocery Stores

There are a lot more restrictions when it comes to selling to grocery stores than most other places. Make sure you know what the regulations are and what your state expects of you before you try to get your veggies, fruits, herbs, and other products on the grocery store shelves. You don't want to get shut down for something that could have been avoided. If you know the regulations, you will already be informed when you approach the grocery stores, which will help you provide a much more convincing sales pitch.

With this being said, there is definitely a market for organic, fresh produce in grocery stores. There has been a massive rise in popularity in farmers' markets and the like, which has caused more commercial stores to shift by providing organic produce to keep up with this trend and retain customers. This has created a massive opportunity for smaller farmers and growers.

The best place to start is by approaching smaller grocers. They will be more open to buying your goods as opposed to much larger grocery store chains. The smaller shops are also a lot more approachable, so it will be easier to meet with the person in charge of buying stock. Most of the advice given in the previous section about approaching restaurants and chefs still applies here. Be prepared and take samples along with you. Do your research and find out what they sell and what they are missing to try and fill this gap.

When selling to grocery stores, you will probably be required to label your food and create branding and signage. Prepare this in advance so that your products are memorable in a good way, and there is an easy association for customers. It will also make you seem more professional.

You could also try selling to schools, hospitals, and any other places that have a cafeteria set up. Don't get discouraged if you get a no from the first few grocers. That happens to everyone, and it will happen to you. Just get back up and try again. It may take quite a few tries before someone says yes. Remember, you are new to the market and still have to build up your credibility and influence.

Selling at Farmers Markets

Farmers' markets are probably the easiest place to get into to sell your goods. Instead of going out and finding customers, the customers come to you. However, that does not mean it is going to be easy. You will have to do some research and make sure that you are prepared for what is to come.

Every farmer's market is different, so make sure you have visited the market that you are keen on joining. Check out the culture, vibe, and competition. See if you can offer something different from what is already there: you want to stand out to attract customers to your booth. Most markets have vendor fees you need to pay to rent a space at the market. Smaller markets usually require smaller fees, so they might be a good place to start.

When you have a booth, everything relies on you, so you need to be organized. You will need a system to keep track of what you have sold and what you still have available. Create an easy to use spreadsheet so you can quickly tick or jot down as you go. In the same vein of being organized, make sure your stand looks appealing, and everything is easily accessible; the prices of each item should also be visible. If things are neat and attractive, people will more likely stop by. Place the best-looking goods out in front or on top. Remember how we chatted about branding and signage in the grocery store section? That comes in handy here as well: good branding will attract people and help them remember you the next time they are at the farmers market.

Once you have attracted people to your stall with your goods and attractive decor and signage, it is now your time to shine. People will rather buy something from someone friendly and talkative. It will also cause them to pause by your stall a while longer. Make sure you are informed and can answer any questions your customers may ask. Give them helpful tips and even recipes and ideas for what to do with what they have just bought. All of this will help you build relationships with your customers, and they will be more likely to come back again.

CB Nuts Story

Here is a story of successful entrepreneurship from someone I met years ago. While working at a business as a sales manager in Bothell Washington, I met Clark Bowen. He ran a business delivering helium tanks, and we were one of his customers. We would bump into each other over the next few years, and one day while walking to a Seattle Mariners game, and there he was, selling fresh roasted peanuts outside the stadium. I loved the freshly roasted smell and bought a bag, of course. Actually, I think he gave them to my family and me "on the house." Clark had always been a startup kind of guy, and I thought I would share their story as it could inspire you in your ventures, as it did me.

CB's Nuts started with a light bulb moment after buying a bag of roasted peanuts from a vendor outside a Mariners-Orioles baseball game in Baltimore. Clark Bowen (CB) had eaten a lot of peanuts on his baseball trip that summer, but there was something about the smell and flavor of these fresh roasted peanuts that captured his attention — this was a unique product you didn't find in his native Pacific Northwest, and he imagined himself learning the craft and selling Mariners and Seahawks fans a better peanut in Seattle.

Soon CB was pushing a small barrel roaster to Safeco Field, and at the time, Quest Field, selling peanuts fresh and hot. At first, he was just hoping to make enough money to pay for tickets to the game and to buy a few $8 beers inside, but finding there were a lot of people eager for his product, he knew he had found his calling. Shortly after, CB met Tami, who became his wife and partner in business, and together they've built CB's from the sidewalk up.

Today, CB's Nuts sells the freshest nuts and seeds to folks all over the world, grown only by American farmers and produced in Kingston, Washington. Our goal is simple, make healthy and delicious snacks for our customers, grown by the best USA farmers, using only simple ingredients.

They also are a great example of responsible business:

"CB's Nuts believes strongly that as a corporation, we are a steward for our community and the environment."

- We pack our peanut butter in reusable/recyclable glass jars.

- Our product is proudly palm oil-free. Learn More about the importance of saying no to palm oil.

- We give 1% of profits from web sales to the Beecher's Foundation.

- We value our employees as our most valuable asset and treat them with respect and honor.

Chapter 7:
Canning, Preserving, and Dehydrating

When growing fresh produce, the worry is always that you will have more than you can use, and it feels terrible if it goes to waste. The good news is that you do not have to get rid of the food you grow if you cannot eat it right away. There are many ways in which you can preserve your food at home. People in generations before us used to preserve their foods all the time: it seems as though this is a skill we have lost, and I think it's time we bring it back.

Benefits for the Family

There are quite a few benefits to preserving your fresh foods. Most fruit, vegetables, and herbs are only available at certain times of the year, which means you will not get to enjoy them when they are out of season. Preserving will also cut down on waste since you will not have to throw away the fresh food you cannot use. Preserving solves many problems and still keeps the food quality, it will just be in a different texture.

Think about how much canned and frozen food you buy regularly. I would imagine that it is quite a substantial amount. You could be saving money on these foods by preserving them yourself. That will cut down how much money you spend on groceries by a reasonable amount. Some preservation techniques do require equipment, but you will easily make that money back in savings.

If you get your kids together, this can be a great time to bond. You can make jellies and jams with the kids and try various recipes for different foods. Kids will be very interested in the whole process, and it will help you bond with them and create memories. Eating the food will be a more enjoyable and delicious experience if they were involved in making it.

Speaking of delicious food, another benefit of preserving your own food is that you are in control of the taste. The flavor is up to you so you can cater to your tastes specifically. Some store-bought preserved foods do not taste the best, and they tend to have way too many additives that bring down the nutritional value. When you do the preserving yourself, you have complete control over what goes into the food and, ultimately, what goes into your body.

On a slightly different note, preserved foods can make a great gift. People will appreciate gifts that you have put effort into, plus there is nothing better than an edible gift. If you are someone who doesn't like to go to someone's house empty-handed, you will be saving quite a bit of money by giving these homemade gifts to your friends and family when you visit them.

Canning

Canning goods dramatically increases the shelf life of many kinds of fruit and vegetables. Two main methods are used to do this: some foods are better canned a certain way, so when you pick the canning method, you have to take what food you are canning into consideration. Any food you will can with an acidic liquid, like pickles, can be canned using the water bath method. All alkaline foods must be canned using a pressure canner.

These methods require you to get some equipment, although the pressure canning methods require more heavy-duty equipment.

Hot Water Bath Method

With this method, you can preserve foods such as jams, jellies, and pickles. You can maintain items for about a year with this method, so it increases your food's shelf life. You will need a few things to get started, namely canning jars, lids, bands, a large pot, a wire rack that fits in the pot, a plastic spatula, a funnel, a lid wand, and a jar lifter. You can get all of this equipment from Amazon or most hardware and kitchen appliance stores.

Once you have all the equipment, you can get started with the canning process. Make sure the jars and all other equipment are properly cleaned. Place the jars in simmering water; this keeps the jars warm to not break when placed in the boiling water bath. The lids also have to be placed in simmering water; this will activate the vacuum seal. You will need to purchase new lids every time you can new items. For both the jars and the lids, make sure the water does not go above 180 degrees Fahrenheit. Fill up the jars with the food you want to preserve. Use the funnel to make this easier. There should be about a ½ inch space between the food and the lid. Take your spatula and run it around the jar's edges to ensure that any air bubbles that have formed are released. Make sure that there is nothing on the rim of the jars by carefully wiping them. Place the bands and the lids on the jars, and tighten until you feel resistance.

Now that the food you want to preserve is in the jars, you will need to place them in the boiling water. It is best to have prepared this pot a bit in advance, so as soon as your jars are filled, you can place them into the pot. The water should be at a rolling boil, lower the jars into the water, placing them onto the wire rack in the pot. The jars should be completely submerged with at least one to two inches of water. Cover and let the jars sit in the water for ten minutes if they are 4 to 12-ounce jars and 15 minutes for 16-ounce jars. Please switch off the heat and let the jars sit in the water for about ten more minutes before removing them from the water.

Remove the jars from the water and place them on a towel. Please make sure that there are at least two inches of space between them. Leave them to cool for at least 12 hours, but it is advisable to leave them 24 hours. Check that the jars have been entirely sealed by testing that the lid does not pop up when pressed. You can remove the band and very lightly try to open the cans. If they have not opened, then they have been appropriately sealed. If any of the jars are still open, you can refrigerate them for a few weeks or freeze for about a year.

Pressure Canning

Pressure canning involves getting the right equipment. You will need a pressure canner, a piece of equipment that can heat the jars to a higher temperature than boiling water. The jars need to be hotter than boiling water because that is what it takes to kill harmful bacteria spores and keep your food safe. The water bath method does not need extreme temperatures because the acidity of the foods kills the spores. That is why the pressure canning method to preserve food is used for ingredients that do not have high acidity.

Pressure canners can vary slightly, but they do have the same structure and build for the most part. A standard pressure canner will have a jar rack, dial gauge, steam vent, and a safety fuse. Each will come with specific instructions on how to use it and navigate the components, so make sure to read the instructions thoroughly before moving on to canning your food.

You may be thinking that pressure canning is going to be complicated, but it isn't. Once you do it the first time, you will get the hang of it and will be able to do it from memory the second time around. The first thing you will need to do is fill the pressure canner with water (follow the specific instructions for your canner to find out how much water you need to add) and place it on the stove to heat up. Place the wire rack into the pressure canner. You can now set the filled jars into the canner, follow the instructions given in the hot water bath method section for the jars' preparation, and how to close them properly.

Once the jars are placed into the pressure canner, you can close the lid and secure it. Turn the heat up and let it boil. Steam should be escaping through the vent. Let this continue for about ten minutes, and after that time has elapsed, close up the vent port. In a few minutes, the canner should come up to pressure. As soon as it has reached the right pressure, you can begin timing. Depending on the food and the size of the jars, the time will range between 5 to 15 minutes. Turn the heat off and let the canner vent; once done, you can open it and remove your jars. Place them on a towel and allow them to cool for about 12 hours or more. You can enjoy your food whenever you are ready. The canned foods can last about a year.

Dehydrating

Dehydrating food is one of the oldest food preservation methods out there, and the generations before us were not wrong about its usefulness. It is actually a very healthy form of preserving food. While some of the food's nutritional value diminishes with canning, this is not as big of a dehydrating problem. You will also be saving space when you dehydrate your foods, as you can fit a lot of food in a small amount of space.

There are also other benefits. For example, you can use this method to make spices and spice mixes. If you dehydrate celery, you can grind it up into a powder and use that to flavor your food instead of using fresh celery. You also have more control over portions. You don't have to open a new bottle or can to use what you need. Please keep it in a large tub or bag, and use what you need each time.

How to

Different types of fresh food have slightly different methods you can use to prepare them and dehydrate them. You may have to go more in-depth for specific fruit and vegetables, but I will give you a general overview to get started. In terms of equipment, you can use an oven, or if you are looking to do this often, you can invest in a dehydrator. If you live in a place with the ideal climate, you can also leave your produce out in the sun and air to dry. With this method, keep checking your food to ensure that no unwanted bugs and flies hang around.

Fruit

Dehydrated fruit makes for great snacks that are easily accessible and healthy. That is perfect for those who have a sweet tooth, as dried fruit tends to have a higher sweetness factor than fresh fruit. The fruit will all have a different texture depending on the type of fruit. You will notice that some fruit like mangoes and guava end up being leathery, and some fruit like bananas turn out crisp.

The time in which the fruit dries varies greatly from fruit to fruit. Dehydrating removes the water and liquid from your produce (or other food items), so for example, fruit with a higher water content will take longer to dry out. The times vary between 4 hours to 24 hours, with stone fruit taking the longest to dry.

The first thing you will need to do is cut all your fruit in even pieces or slices. That will allow the pieces to dry at the same time. Fruit tends to go brown during the drying process. If you want to prevent a large amount of browning, treat the fruit with a lemon juice dip. Mix one cup of lemon juice to one quart of water, place the fruit in the mixture for about five minutes, and then remove and put it on the drying rack. It is better to use a rack than a tray: the rack will allow the air to circulate around the fruit more evenly, but you are more than welcome to use a tray if you wish.

You might have to play with the temperature a bit since each fruit will vary, but in general, you can use 125 to 135 degrees Fahrenheit as a guide. Some fruit prefers lower temperatures, but you can use a higher temperature initially and then bring it down; this works if you are using either a dehydrator or oven. Leave enough space between each piece of fruit so that the air can circulate properly. Drying may begin with the skin on or off. That is up to personal preference unless you are drying fruit like bananas, in which case you must remove the skin.

Vegetables

Dehydrated vegetables dry a bit differently than fruit, but similar principles apply. The vegetables will dry crispy and should not be bendy or leathery when dried. The drying time can vary between four to 14 hours; this depends on the vegetable's water content. Dehydrated vegetables can flavor food and also be used as spices: they will increase your dishes' flavor intensity. You can also have them as chips since they get crunchy. For example, zucchini chips are incredibly delicious.

Cut your vegetables in thin, even slices. You will need to blanch each piece. Blanching is done by placing the vegetables in a pot of boiling water for a short time, then removing them and immersing in iced water. Once you have done this, you can place them on a rack. The best way to dry out the vegetables is to use a dehydrator, or you can place them in the sun. You may use the oven, but this can be ineffective in some cases.

The temperature in which you dehydrate may also vary depending on the vegetables. Vegetables with high water content like tomatoes will need a higher temperature, about 145 degrees Fahrenheit. Most other vegetables can dehydrate at 125 degrees Fahrenheit. Make sure that there is space between each piece since you want the air to circulate evenly. Once they have fully dehydrated, you can place them in a container or even blend them into a powder to use as a spice or flavor enhancer.

Herbs

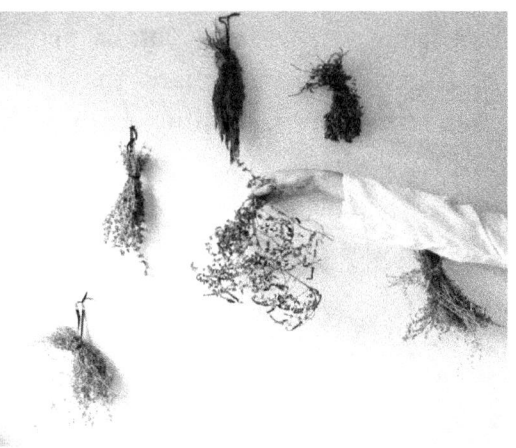

Herbs are fantastic when added to food, but sometimes it is hard to keep them fresh, so it is best to dry them out. Dried herbs retain their flavor relatively well, as most of us know, since dried herbs are a staple in most kitchens.

There are two ways to dry your herbs: you can hang them up by their stems and let them dry naturally, or you can take the leaves off the stems and dry them like that. You do not need to use a dehydrator since the water content is already relatively low in a herb. Either method works for almost all herbs and spices, but remember to rinse them well before drying them out.

If you want to leave them on the stems, the first thing you need to do is take your herbs and divide them into smaller bunches. You will probably have a considerable amount of herbs, and smaller bunches will dry quicker. You can tie them together with string, rubber bands, or anything else you think will work. Place the herbs in a brown bag to prevent anything from getting on them. Now hang them upside down from somewhere the sun can reach them, likely by a window.

It will take a few days for the herbs to dry out, but the exact time depends on your climate. Once they are dry, you can remove them from the stems by just crunching them off. Place them in an airtight jar or container. Just watch your container, and if you notice that there is condensation happening on the sides of the glass.

That means that the herbs need to dry out more. If this is the case, just place them on a tray and leave them uncovered for approximately two days. It is best to leave them to dry as long as possible initially so that you do not have to do this step.

The other method requires you to remove the leaves from the stems and place them on a dry tray. You will need to cover the leaves with a cheesecloth and leave it in a warm, dark place. It will take a few days for the herbs to dry out. These choices just come down to your personal preference.

Freezing

We will quickly talk about freezing, as it is probably the simplest method of preserving food. Food usually lasts about two or three months in the freezer, and this method works best when you are keeping the food for yourself. Selling frozen food can be a bit tricky: if you want to go down that route, remember that you will not be able to keep a large stock for very long periods.

Freezing food for your family is undoubtedly the most straightforward form of food preservation. It makes it easy for people who have busy schedules to cook at the start of the week and keep food in the freezer to thaw out and enjoy when pressed for time or unable to cook from scratch. That is a more efficient way of preparing meals, and we see it being adopted by many people.

Cooked food is not the only thing that can be frozen: you can also freeze your fresh produce. That is a great way to lock in the flavor and nutrients of ripe fruit and vegetables. Frozen fruit and veg can keep for up to a year in the freezer, and when you thaw out most vegetables, they retain their texture. If you are not keen on thawing the produce out, you can just use them straight from frozen. Throw frozen fruit into a blender and make delicious smoothies, or even pop them straight into your mouth: frozen berries are incredibly delicious. Frozen vegetables can be put directly on the stove to cook, no need to thaw in most cases. They are an excellent addition to your soups and stews in the winter months.

For the best results when freezing, blanch your fruit and vegetables before freezing them: this will help them retain their color and texture. Be cautious because they can stick together when freezing, making it challenging to use going forward. It is best to lay your fruit or vegetables out on a tray, freeze them, and then place them into your containers or freezer bags. That works for all produce except for leafy greens, which usually don't freeze well. You can try cooking them down and then freezing them, but in my experience, it's not possible to get leafy greens to retain a fresh texture when freezing them.

When freezing your food, make sure that it is fresh and clean. Unlike canning, freezing does not destroy any spores or bacteria on the food. It will only stop it from growing. So if your food is going off when you put it into the freezer, it will come out the same way, and you will have only paused the process.

Selling Possibilities

Selling preserved produce is a bit harder than selling fresh and baked goods. It is not impossible, but there is quite a bit more red tape that you will have to get over to do it. Make sure you check with your local authorities before you move forward.

Dried herbs are more uncomplicated to sell than other foods in most states, and you probably do not need a permit to do so. However, most other foods do have some regulations around them. If you are interested in selling cottage foods (foods that are homemade: this includes cookies, some candies, some canned foods, and other non-perishables), you might have to register with the local government and be issued with a certificate to allow you to sell the food. You can refer back to the links in Chapter 6 to see the requirements for you to sell certain foods and produce.

Chapter 8:
Greener Driving for You, and Delivery for Your Business

I'm sure you have heard of the many changes coming for the automobile and transportation in general. Greener driving is mentioned in articles by advocates frequently, while the products themselves have been slow to market. There have been many innovations and incentives for moving the manufacturers and consumers in this "new" direction. The goal of green driving is to lessen the impact that traveling has on the environment. Emissions of cars and trucks cause significant air pollution on the road: most of us have cars or use some sort of transport to get around, nearly gone are the days of walking and riding our bikes to work.

We won't soon be rid of our cars and other transportation modes; that would not be feasible. But society is moving in that direction. More and more people want at least a hybrid vehicle for the next car they purchase. And get ready for a massive wave of electric vehicles from

Volkswagon, Nissan, General Motors, etc. I think the new V.W. Bus due out in 2023 with be a huge success! Electric trucks are coming from Ford, Tesla, and other manufacturers. A rugged hybrid Jeep Wrangler is coming out in early 2021, getting 25 miles on electricity and then gasoline from there. No manufacturer wants to be left behind. Here is a question, what do you drive? What should you be driving? P.S. I am considering a new VW ID 4 (Google it!) to replace the Chevy Volt I have had for seven years.

E-bikes

E-bikes are precisely what they sound like, electric bikes. You may have seen them buzzing around your neighborhood. They are similar to regular bicycles, but they have a battery and a motor that assists you with your ride. We all know that riding a bike to a destination is much more environmentally friendly than taking your car. However, the downside is that riding your bike for long distances ends up leaving you tired and sweaty before you even get to your destination: this is not ideal, especially if you are traveling to work. The e-bike helps you pedal so that you do not turn up to your destination, looking like you have just completed the Tour de France.

That is an especially good option if you won't often travel long distances, so if you work relatively close to home, this will work for you. The battery and motor system do not entirely power these bikes. Remember, these bikes assist you and not do all the work for you, so you will also be getting some exercise. That is a positive in my book. I think we could all use a bit more activity in our lives. I know I could!

There are lots of options to choose from if you are interested in purchasing an e-bike. They vary in functionality and build, with some relying more heavily on the motor than others. Whichever you prefer, there is an option out there for you. The bikes fall into a few categories, namely hybrid, road, and folding bikes. Whichever you choose, they all lessen the amount of work you have to do to get from point A to point B and help you carry heavier loads without breaking a sweat.

Hybrid bikes are the most popular option as they offer a mix between two extremes. They can handle roads as well as park tracks but still provide comfort. They are a good option if you are looking for an excellent day-to-day bike: they may not be the fastest, but that is neither here nor there when considering that they get the job done and are sturdy.

The road bike category is faster than the hybrid variety. The focus is to keep the bike's weight low, so the designers have dropped handlebars to assist with this. They can be enjoyable to ride, but make sure you keep to the speed limit when on the road. These do have the power to exceed it. These bikes also handle hills pretty well.

The folding bike is one that probably looks less like a regular bike than the others. The folding capability makes them great if you commute to work using public transport, as you can quickly fold up your bike to get on and off public transport with it. They're also a good option if you have limited space at your home or wherever you work. Besides that, these bikes are still comfortable to ride and can get the job done.

Electric and Hybrid Cars

Electric cars run only on electricity: you plug them in to charge them, and then off you go. You can download apps on your phone that show where charging stations are, and many electric cars will guide you on the car's navigation screen. While a mix of electricity and gas fuels hybrid cars, they are still considered green cars because they have better internal combustion that allows them to be more efficient and run cleaner. Ultimately the goal is just that, to have vehicles that run clean and can get us to our destinations without negatively affecting the environment.

If you are looking for an excellent electric or hybrid car, there are a few options, and many are not too expensive. One of the best ones to consider is the Nissan Leaf: this is a fully electric car, and if you purchase a newer model, then the mileage can go up to 149 miles for a full 40 kWh battery or 226 miles for a 62 kWh battery (Nissan USA, 2019). The battery does lose some range over time, but this should be expected over several years. Check the manufacturer's warranty and see how the car is doing near the end of the battery coverage. Often batteries have coverage of 8 years or 100.000 miles. The factory will not guarantee full range until the end of that period, asking to read the warranty before taking the plunge is a good idea! As the end of your coverage approaches, you can check your range compared to when it was new. You can also see how much a replacement battery is, and see the latest models you could be tempted to consider trading!

To install a home charger if needed, you can utilize various electricians, and even Amazon Home Services to install an electric charger on your property: they provide vetted electricians that can help you with any queries along the process. You can access more information on this by following this link: <u>Nissan Leaf Charging Solutions: Home & Business Services</u>.

Every year Forbes comes out with a list of the top green cars for the year. These cars are given a green score that shows the environmental friendliness of the vehicle. This score is called the Environmental Damage Index (EDX). I believe that car battery recycling will help on the "front end" of the manufacturing process with time. The green score considers the whole car life cycle, from manufacturing to being put on the road and driven. That gives an accurate indication of the environmental impact the cars have. Using this information, they can rank the best environmentally friendly cars on the market. For this year (2020), the vehicles that have come out on top are the Toyota Prius Prime Plug-in Hybrid, the Kia Niro Hybrid, the Toyota Prius Eco Hybrid, Hyundai Ioniq Electric, the Honda Insight Hybrid, and the BMW i3 Electric (Gorzelany, 2020). There are a few others, but this list just shows you that there is a variety to choose from and both hybrid and fully electric options from which to choose.

CNG Cars and Vans

CNG stands for compressed natural gas. These cars and vans use this as fuel instead of the more common petroleum-based fuels most other vehicles use. These cars are more fuel-efficient, and they release fewer emissions than the alternative. There are pros and cons to driving a CNG vehicle, so you will have to decide whether this is the right fit for you.

The big bonuses are that fuel is cheaper, and it is better for the environment. Natural gases are abundant: that means that the fuel for CNG cars is less expensive than petroleum-based fuels. You can also find inexpensive used CNG cars as they are not widely considered as an option for consumer use outside of government fleets. They are not even widely known about by the average consumer. I saw several on GovDeals.com available to bid on! The environment benefits from this type of power since it has a 90 to 97% reduced carbon-monoxide emission and a 35 to 60% reduced nitrogen-oxide emission. That is quite a significant decline in emissions (Compare.com, 2018).

These cars drive and look the same as regular cars, so you do not feel the difference from day to day. Some examples of this type of car are the Fiat Panda Panda 1.4 8v Natural Power, the Ford Focus CNG, the Mercedes-Benz B 180 NGT, and the Opel Zafira 1.6 CNG ecoFLEX Turbo. Suppose you are looking to get a van to help out with your business. In that case, some good options are the IVECO Daily CNG, the Fiat

Ducato Natural Power, the Mercedes-Benz Sprinter NGT, and the Fiat Doblo 1.6 Natural Power.

The one thing that you will have to consider when getting a CNG vehicle is where to fill up with gas. Unfortunately, CNG is not as commonly available as regular gas. Many stations cater to CNG cars, but you will have to make sure that you live in an area where CNG stations are accessible. Check out this map of CNG filling stations to see if there are ones placed conveniently for you: Alternative Fuels Data Center: Natural Gas Fueling Station Locations.

Chapter 9: Selling Carbon Neutral Services and Products Online

There are so many ways to make money online. Online business and online earning potential have grown considerably over the past few years. You can do everything from the comfort of your own home, as long as you have a laptop and an internet connection. Not only is this convenient for you, but it is also good for the environment. These jobs do not take up many resources and can be close to carbon-neutral because they are mainly online. So not only do they provide you with extra income, but they are also environmentally friendly.

Teaching and Tutoring

If there is a subject that you are particularly good at or something you enjoy doing, why not use that skill to earn some money? Many online tutoring sites allow you to teach from the comfort of your own home. Every platform works differently, but they all allow for flexible work schedules, so you can get online when you are available to teach. Hourly rates will also vary depending on the platform, subject, and the level of difficulty of the subject being taught.

It is very gratifying to teach someone something and help them understand a subject where they struggle. Think back to your school days, don't you wish there had been someone available to help you when you needed an extra hand? You can be that person for someone else. Some subjects and platforms require you to have a degree, but many do not have the same requirement. So look into what you can teach, given your educational background and skill set.

You can look at a few websites and online tutoring platforms if you are interested in going down this route:

• Chegg Tutors - Online Tutoring Jobs

• Wyzant - Wyzant: Find Private Tutors at Affordable Prices, In-Person & Online

• Tutor.com - Online Tutoring, Homework Help and Test Prep in Math, Science, and English - Tutor.com

Selling Your Products Online

Online platforms are a great way to get the word out about your product. Selling products online has become much more accessible and will cost you a minimal amount compared to regular businesses. It is probably the easiest way to get your products sold as long as you follow the guidelines set out by each platform.

Whether you use someone else's platform or your own, you will need to market your product effectively to get people interested and wanting to buy your product. Put up attractive and clear pictures of your product, as people want to see what they are buying. If you can put up multiple images, then do so, customers will be more trusting if they can see what you are offering correctly. Also, make sure the description of the product is comprehensive and precise. People do not have direct access to you when online shopping, so you want to think about what questions they may have and answer them in the description. Let's take a look at some of the platforms you can utilize to sell your products.

eBay

eBay is one of the biggest platforms to sell your products, with over 182 million buyers on this online marketplace (Roizen, 2019). If you're looking for customers, this is the right place to start. You can sell used items as long as they are in good condition and new things that you have made yourself. eBay also has a few cool tools that will help you to be successful at getting your items sold.

To effectively sell your products, you will need to know when the right time to sell is and at what price you should sell your items. You can use the Trending now tool to find out what things are trending and when they became a trend. Another useful tool on eBay is the What it's worth tool; this will show you the prices of similar items. Using it, you will find out how much people are willing to spend on specific merchandise, and you can price your products accordingly.

You have two options on eBay: you can sell using the auction-style or the fixed price selling option. The auction-style selling works best when you are selling unique, antique, or more expensive items. The fixed price option is better for homemade items that you can sell at lower prices. Remember to consider shipping prices: most people do not want to spend large amounts of money on shipping. It is much more popular to have low-priced or free shipping.

You will need to add as many keywords in the title and description of your product so people can easily find it. Think about ways that people might search for your item or a similar item. Please take a look at how others have written out their product names and descriptions. It will be no use having a terrific piece of merchandise on the market if no one can find it.

Shopify

Shopify is one of the largest e-commerce sites in the world. It does require you to purchase a subscription package to set up a shop. There are different package levels, so you need to choose the one that best suits you. There is a free trial that allows you to sell fifty items and then upgrade to a full subscription. Once you have acquired your subscription, you will need to set up your shop: this is a pretty simple process, and the interface is easy to navigate.

The good thing about Shopify is that your shop could show up on the Google page when someone types in something while they are searching for products like yours. You will be able to tweak what people see on the Google search page as well. That can extend your reach, but there is no guarantee that your page will show up on the Google search page. Your 'shop' will list everything you are selling, so once someone clicks into the website, they will see everything you have to offer. Remember to add good quality pictures and descriptions for each product.

Shopify lets you design your shop and pick themes that will make it pleasing to navigate through. The number of options you have depends on the package you have chosen; more expensive packages will come with a lot more options. There are also various plugins you could add that will make it a more pleasurable experience to shop in. If you are looking to have a permanent place to sell multiple products, Shopify is an excellent way to go. You can visit Sell products online with Shopify to get that free trial of Shopify and see if it may work for you.

Etsy and Printful

Etsy is another website where you can set up a shop and sell your items. It is a pretty large e-commerce website that specializes in vintage, homemade, and unique items. That's what differentiates this platform from others. Everyone who searches on here will be looking for something custom or handmade, so you might get a better response selling your homemade goods here than anywhere else. You can also set up your shop for free on Etsy: just be aware of the listing, checkout, and other fees.

You will need to differentiate yourself from the average seller on the platform to stand out. It is a huge platform, so the chances of someone else selling something similar to yours are relatively high. Think about making yourself stand out somehow, whether in the way you package your products or through something unique about the product itself. You also want to make sure that you price your products correctly: you can look at what others are charging for similar products.

Etsy collaborates with Printful: you can design and make something on Printful and sell it on Etsy. Printful specializes in clothing, accessories, and even home items. That makes it even easier for you to make a business out of selling on Etsy. However, just as we stated before, you will have to make your products stand out. The competition can be quite stiff, so make yours as unique as possible.

Amazon FBA

Fulfillment by Amazon (FBA) is intended to help sellers streamline their processes. Many sellers do not have the warehouse space or manpower to package their products and send them off on time to their customers. So Amazon does this for you: you send your products to an Amazon fulfillment center, and the Amazon staff takes care of the storing, packaging, and shipping of your products to the customer.

That is a great benefit to you because it takes all the stress out of doing everything yourself. Plus, people will be more trusting of the items because of the Amazon name. Another great thing about Amazon FBA is that it can handle the products sold on multiple platforms, so you are not just restricted to selling on Amazon.

Of course, all of this is not available for free: there is a fee involved, so you have to keep that in mind when using it. The fees that you can expect to pay are seller fees, fulfillment fees, storage fees, and if you are shipping overseas international shipping fees will apply. Also, be aware that you will have to adhere to the product guidelines set out by

Amazon because they are putting their name on the line; this is to be expected.

Of course, there are pros and cons to this service, but it is up to you to decide whether it is right for you. The convenience of it all is definitely the best part, but if you have a minimal amount of products you are selling, it may not be worth it, so weigh up the options and see if this something you would like to look into.

Blogging

This one is a little different from the rest because you can sell and promote products using a blog, but that requires you to start a blog. Also, having a blog itself can earn you money if you are willing to put in the work. You will probably not make any money for the first year or more after starting your blog, but staying committed is the key to success. I will take you through the basics of creating your blog, but the actual content and what goes in will be up to you.

There are a few platforms that you can use to start your blog, but WordPress is by far the most popular. It is also one of the most comfortable places to navigate if you want to create a website or blog. Before you even get into setting up your website, you will need to decide on a niche: this should be small enough to keep you focused and broad enough to have content to write about.

144

Next, you will need to think of a name for your blog and a domain name for your website: if it is possible to get these two to be related or the same, that would be ideal. Try and get a .com domain name as these will get the most exposure compared to country-specific extensions.

After you have done all that, you will need to choose a hosting provider and install WordPress. There are many hosting providers out there but just Googling "WordPress hosting providers" should bring up a few options for you to choose from. A majority of hosting providers will have a plugin for you to install WordPress.

The next two steps are also technical: configure Accelerated Mobile Projects pages and set up Google Analytics. There are excellent guides on the internet for both, and a simple Google search will lead you to the right information.

As you can see, there is a lot more to setting up a blog than just pushing out content. But once you get to this point, you can finally start writing. The writing you will need to be doing to get traffic onto your site will have to be keyword focused pieces. You want people who search for specific things to stumble upon your page. Don't get discouraged if you do not have an influx of readers early on in the process, keep at it, and stick to your niche. Once you have done this, you can decide on how you want to monetize your blog. Again this won't be initially, but when your blog gains some traction, you can start making marketing decisions. You could sell your products, become an affiliate, or run ads for other companies and pages. That is up to you, but make sure you choose what works best for you, your situation, and goals.

Homemade Items

Now that we have discussed how we can sell our products, we should move on to what we can sell. When thinking about selling a product online, think about what you enjoy doing and what you are good at. This way, you will enjoy making the products, and you will want to continue doing it for a while. I have put together a few ideas for you if you are stuck, but don't feel limited by these. You are free to branch out and explore many different items and avenues. You can use the platforms mentioned in the previous section or create your website to get your business off the ground.

Candles

Candles are among the easiest things to make for the home, and many people will pay good money. They add to the ambiance of a room by giving it a sense of calm and romance. Candle-making does not require much from you. All you need to get started with standard candles are wax, wicks, containers, coloring, fragrances, and a pot to melt the wax.

Take the wax, coloring (you can use food coloring), and fragrance (essential oils work well), place everything into a pot over a stove to heat up. You may want to heat the wax first then slowly add the coloring and fragrance. This way, it is easier to see and control the amounts you are adding. You can also use old candles and old wax shavings; this way, you are recycling!

After these have melted together, you have two options: you can pour the wax into a container or use the candle dipping method. The container option is far simpler and quicker. Just make sure you pick a fire-safe container, and pretty to look at. Glass mason jars work perfectly for this. If you want to try candle dipping, you will need to weigh your wick to keep it straight: a metal bolt works perfectly. Take the wick and dip it in the wax, remove and wait for it to dry. Once dry, repeat the process as many times as desired: once the candle is heavy enough, you can cut the weight off.

Soaps

The best way to go about this as a beginner will be to buy a premade soap base, which will let you practice with different colors and scents efficiently. There are ways to make soap from scratch, and recipes are available online, both using lye and without it. For now, we will just focus on using the premade soap base. You can purchase the soap base, called melt or pour base, from soap shops and online platforms like Amazon.

Once you have your base, cut it up into small chunks and melt it down over a slow heat. Add in a few drops of essential oil: if you want to use any, coloring makes sure it is skin safe and non-staining. Once melted together, you can pour the mixture into silicone molds of your choice. You can decorate your soap by adding dried herbs and fruit or even cut a sponge and place it in to dry in the soap, then package as desired.

Art and Crafts

If you enjoy doing crafts, then why not make some money from it. Try designing things like bookmarks, journals, or keep it simple and paint or draw beautiful pictures if you're artistically inclined. People love it when items are personalized, so use this to your advantage, have specific designs, and request words, names, messages, and colors they would like to have added to their product.

Sewing, Knitting, and Wearable Items

There is always a market for unique wearable items. They do not have to be items like shirts and pants. Try going for more simple things like scarves, pocket squares, handkerchiefs, headbands, and cloth face masks. If you are good at this kind of craft, it shouldn't take too long to make a batch and get it ready for selling. You should look at what is trendy at the moment and then give it a slightly different spin to make it attractive to people but also unique.

Beaded bracelets and necklaces are also quite popular. You can add a personalization option to your crafts by adding birthstones or something similar to the design. Depending on the materials you use, jewelry can be pretty inexpensive to make. Creating jewelry allows you to be creative and design things that you think are beautiful, and others will enjoy wearing. You can sell the jewelry you make individually or as a pack of as many as you like. Think about using attractive packaging to make them even more appealing, as customers always appreciate this.

Food Items

There is quite a lot of red tape around selling food products online: that is not to say it is impossible, but it is more complicated than marketing other products. Be prepared for this if you want to sell food items online. The reason for this is that food items can be more dangerous for consumers than other things since food is consumed: the laws and regulations around selling food are there for the protection of the consumer.

Dried herbs and herbal products might be a little easier to get through, but you will have to check your specific state's regulations on this. For the most part, make sure that whatever you are selling meets FDA regulations, and that any claims you make about the product are factual. You might be shut down if they find out that you are not living up to what you are promising. That also comes down to integrity, so be honest and do your research, and you should be fine.

Gift or Subscription Boxes

Pretty boxes containing different goodies have taken off in the past few years. We see lots of websites and brands doing boxes with other samples and gifts. There are two ways in which you can do a goodie box: you could sell them as a once-off gift box, or you could sell a subscription box service.

The gift boxes will work whether you have your own website or not, but it will be easier for the customer to personalize them if you have a website. The first thing you will need to do is think about what you will be putting in the box: picking a theme is the best way to do this. You want your package to be coherent and not just have a bunch of random stuff inside. The theme could be color specific, or if you are doing food items, you could pick a flavor, or even just things that go with a particular event or part of the house. For example, if you were going to do a gift box, the theme could be lavender or things you can bathe with. There could be candles, a bath sponge, soap, a bath bomb, and cream in the box. People love buying these boxes because they are a quick and easy gift idea, and just the thought of receiving lots of little things excites people.

If you want to go the subscription box route, you would need your own website or another way for people to subscribe. You could run the subscription service off your blog if you decided to start one. Of course, you would need to have a niche that people would want to subscribe to. For example, I've seen subscription boxes for coffee that send you a new brew, recipe, and coffee utensils every month. By staying subscribed, you eventually end up building a beautiful collection. Another idea for you could be a herb subscription box: every month, you could send your customers a new dried herb, with a food recipe and an alternative way to use the herb. You could even add another ingredient that would pair well with the herb, or write out a little story on a notecard to give it a personal touch. Subscriptions are a great way to get recurring business, and people are more invested in what they subscribe to, so take advantage of that.

Chapter 10:
Skills to Learn for Low Cost or Even FREE!

Expanding your knowledge and education is vital if you want to be successful and better yourself in general. When you gain more experience, you will be able to do more and take on more opportunities as they come. There is no such thing as having too much knowledge.

The thing that stops people from learning and being more educated is that they think it will be expensive. Most people do not have lots of money lying around to pick up a new degree or enroll in expensive classes. The good news is that this is not the only way to learn new skills and gain more knowledge on specific subjects.

Online Studies: The Environmentally Friendly Way to Study

There are plenty of ways to study inexpensively or even for free. The bonus is that these are all online, so you can easily fit it into your schedule. You can play around and try out different platforms. Some instructors have different teaching styles, so find the one that works for you. If you haven't learned a new skill or participated in a class in a long time, do something you truly enjoy first, this will ease you into it. After that, you can pick up subjects that may be a bit tougher and not as fun.

Online Courses

There are so many privately run online courses, in every genre and level. These courses are usually started by people who have degrees and experience in the subjects they are teaching. Some are free, and some you will have to pay a fee for, but that fee will be nowhere as expensive as a formal course or qualification. Think about what you would like to learn and do some digging to find out if someone has a course for that subject. Two suggestions I can give you are for a bookkeeping course and a course on organic gardening. These are both free and can be used to start a business or if you just want to grow personally. Check out the following links to go straight to the courses: <u>Free Online Bookkeeping Course and Training</u> and <u>Free Organic Garden Course from Mike's Green Garden and the Organic Gardener Podcast</u>. The bookkeeping course will help you plan to run your own business: finances are such an essential part of that, and you need to know how to track and spend your money. The organic gardening course is precisely what it sounds like. We went through it in Chapter 5, but you will get a much more in-depth knowledge of the course subject. Plus, someone is speaking directly to you, and you will see what they are doing if anything is unclear in the written format.

Utilize YouTube

I think YouTube is an underutilized tool. Most people just use it for entertainment, which is excellent. We all love a funny and entertaining video, but you can learn many things on this platform. People skilled in specific areas love sharing their knowledge on subjects close to their hearts, and it's all free.

If you have never used YouTube as a learning platform, then you are missing out. All you have to do is type in something that you are interested in, a course name, or name of a skill, and YouTube will show you everything similar that they have on their database. All that's left for you to do is click play and start learning. To give you an example, you could type in 'free gardening class,' and something like this will pop up: Gardening Classes on YouTube.

edX

edX is a great website to take part in professional-level courses and learn skills. Their partners are accredited universities like Berkeley, Harvard, Boston University, MIT, and various others. The classes are very informative and professionally done, and they do not cost as much as a traditional university course. You can learn anything from business management all the way to water governance. These courses are broken down into lessons, and many of them offer tools or exercises to help you through the learning process.

Udemy

Udemy is a favorite when it comes to learning a new skill or just learning something in general. It is one of the largest learning platforms with the widest variety of courses. The courses are rated by past students so you can see whether the results are worth it, plus the prices are often very reasonable. Some studies go for just a few dollars, and they often have sales on popular programs. You can go directly to their website to see the full list of classes available and their prices: Udemy: Online Courses - Learn Anything, On Your Schedule.

It is mostly video content with some at-home exercises, depending on which course you take.

Studies also vary in length and depth of information. The unique thing about this website is that you can make money from it if you have a skill you want to share. There is an option to put up your own course, and you will get paid for it. Of course, people will be reviewing the course, so make sure you do it well and give out useful information.

Tips for Getting More from Your Learning Experience

Once you have picked your course, it is time to start learning. Gaining a new skill will take time and effort, but it will be rewarding, not to mention beneficial: there is always something to gain by expanding your mind to new ideas and concepts. Here are a few tips that can help you get the most out of your studying.

Stay Committed

Like with anything in life, to achieve real results, you will need to be committed. Make sure that you keep going and are consistent. Sometimes it can feel like you aren't making any progress if you only half commit to your studies on and off. Whether it is an easy, fun course or a more severe and in-depth course, the same principle will apply. As soon as you stop being consistent, there will be a higher chance that you will stop and forget about it. And getting restarted is going to be much more challenging if you keep stopping halfway and have to go back to remember what you have already learned.

Stick to a Designated Time and Place

People are creatures of habit. We find it much easier to do things if they are done the same way every time. Sometimes you will not be motivated, and it will help to have habits and routines in place to carry you through that. So pick a designated study place and decide what time you will sit down and get to work.

If you have the same routine, your brain will recognize that it is time to study instead of being distracted by various other things. You will also be more likely to do it if you have already predetermined to do it. It doesn't even have to be a long study session. Some of the courses are relatively short. So whatever amount of time you have available, do it for that time.

Now it does not have to be at the same time every day. Life gets busy, and sometimes every day looks different, but for the most part, you will know what you have to get done at the beginning of the day. When working on your to-do list, make sure you put studying there and pick a time to do it. The more you leave up to chance, the less likely you are to do it.

Stay Focused

One of the biggest mistakes people make when they are studying is letting themselves get distracted. If you want to study smarter, not harder, you will have to be focused on what you are doing. It may be challenging initially, but once you recognize what distracts you, you will avoid it before it has a chance to ruin your study session.

Resist the urge to multitask: it doesn't work. It might seem like a good idea to watch an online course video while cooking, cleaning, or completing another task, but it will take your attention away from learning. Taking 30 minutes of uninterrupted time to study and learn is much more useful than taking two hours to get the information into your head because you were busy with something else.

Social media, or just your phone in general, can be a big distraction. You usually will not need your phone when you are studying, so put it away in another room or put it on silent. We all know that once we are distracted by one thing on social media, we will get sucked in and end up scrolling for hours. Rather avoid this, get your studying done, and then you are free to do whatever you like.

It can be worthwhile to do brief pre-study sessions and post wrap up reviews to remember things much better. Listening to the material after will help you remember the information you have learned. If you choose to do it as pre-study preparation, your mind will be prepared when you sit down and study.

Teach it to Someone Else

One of the best ways to retain knowledge is to teach it to someone else. Now you don't have to put on a full-on lecture, but generally sharing the information you have learned makes it stick in your head. That is partly because you will tell what you don't know and what you know well when you speak it out loud. Another bonus is that now someone else has learned something new. Perhaps you can even film yourself teaching this new skill and upload it to YouTube; you never know who you could reach.

Do the Practical Work

Most of the courses will come with some practical components, and it can be easy to skip portions because no one is there to check up on you. Don't fall into this trap! The practical components are there to make sure you understood the concepts well enough to apply them. There is no point in studying if you cannot use what you have learned.

Even if the course does not have a practical component, make one up for yourself. Are you doing classes on effective seed planting? Get some seeds and practice what you have learned. Often the best way to learn is to try to do the task. You will be able to see what you understand and what you do not. You then have the opportunity to go back to any part you did not understand and do them over again, rather than figuring it out when it's too late.

Once you have successfully done the practical work, you know you are ready to move on. It will also make the next section easier to understand if you fully understand what was previously presented. Plus, the practical parts are probably the most fun, and they are the whole point of doing the course. There is no point in having all this knowledge in your head if you do nothing with it.

Chapter 11:
Making a Difference: Jobs, Businesses and Volunteering Ideas!

No matter who we are or where we are from, we can all make a difference in some capacity, and it is vital that we do what we can. Some of us can make a career shift and move into a job where the environment is the main focus, and some can start a business that focuses on bettering the environment. Others have the time to volunteer and give their time to organizations and initiatives to better the environment. Some of us can make changes in our lives that will lead to living more sustainably and being more environmentally conscious.

In whichever category you fall into, remember that the most important thing is that you are trying and are moving towards being effective in that space. Whether small or big, every change matters. There are always improvements that can be achieved.

Green Jobs

If you are looking to enter a professional space regarding sustainability and protecting the environment, many job opportunities are now available. Many sectors are moving into more environmentally-conscious business plans, that has opened the door for many environmental careers. Some require you to study and get a degree, while others do not. There are many more than what I can mention in this section, but use this list as a base and see if you can explore other green jobs. These examples are provided by National Geographic (2012), and they are the fastest-growing green jobs at the moment.

Urban Farmers/Growers

Now that locally sourced produce has gotten a lot more popular, and people are more conscious of where they get their food from, urban farmers will be an essential part of small economies. Many cities do not have large land spaces to grow produce, but thankfully, solutions like hydroponics and vertical growing large areas are not needed. We have seen some urban growers utilizing space on rooftops to grow fresh produce to supply to local restaurants, farmers' markets, and grocery stores.

Water Quality Technicians

The oceans and other bodies of water are suffering because of pollution. Some of the most critical green jobs deal with the quality of our water sources. These people work towards bringing them back up to a high standard. Water quality technicians develop and implement plans and technology to mitigate pollution, causing a decline in water quality.

Clean Car Engineers

Remember the cars we discussed in Chapter 7? The people designing and building those are engineers who focus on producing sustainable vehicles and use the least amount of energy possible. They implement the solutions that may bring about a decline in pollution due to transportation emissions. If you want to move into something like this, you would need a degree in the field. An easier route would be to work for a dealership as an electric vehicle salesperson. It is much easier representing and selling a product that is part of the solution.

Green Energy Professionals

Alternative energy is so crucial if the world is to move into a more sustainable state. Wind energy and wave energy are two of the energy options that are being explored and implemented. Jobs linked to this are increasing, whether they are scientists or people working at the plants.

Recyclers

As recycling becomes more popular, there needs to be someone there to do the recycling. The people who work for recycling plants perform various functions, from sorting through the material and transporting it to its destination and operating the machinery. We must have people doing these jobs since nothing would be recycled without their help.

Natural Scientists

The only reason we have the information we have now is that someone studied and researched to give us that information. That is such an important job, but you will need an industry-specific degree to pursue something like this. Scientists are in the trenches researching how the environment and those that live in it react to various situations and then develop solutions to their problems.

These scientists monitor and analyze different solutions to make sure they are working. They are the ones who have the most knowledge about subjects linked to the environment. As we move towards a greener world, we will need people who truly understand the science behind everything and can work on developing what we need to get better at implementing greener solutions.

Solar Cell Technicians

We spoke about the importance of solar power in Chapter 3. We also chatted about the innovations that have come about with solar technology: these are the people who are developing and testing that technology. They test the technology's efficacy and see how much solar energy can be absorbed from the sun. They are also the ones who build and produce innovations to better the power generation in solar energy.

We mentioned things like using solar panels on clothing and exposed surfaces. These were all designed by these technicians. They do not only invent new technology but test existing ones. Someone is always there monitoring trends and making sure that what is already in place is running at its best. This kind of job will continue to be in demand in the coming years since more sustainable energy opportunities are emerging.

Start a Recycling Business

A recycling business can be quite lucrative if you do it properly. Most people will think that a recycling business is just about collecting papers and selling them to recycling plants. While this is one way to do it, it is not the only way, nor is it the most lucrative way to start your recycling business.

There are so many items that can be recycled it pays to think outside the box. Most cities and suburbs have paper and maybe plastic and glass recycling programs. Suppose you want to make a lot of money from your business. In that case, you will have to do something different: competing with already well-established companies might be difficult unless you have something unique to offer. You could try scrap metal or collecting old computers to resell parts. You could even start a small business based on re-using old ink cartridges and just refilling them. Recycling does not have only to be taking materials to a recycling plant; there are many ways to recycle.

If you are looking to collect recyclable materials from your community for recycling plants, you will have to look to make it convenient for others. People won't do something if it is too much work. See if you can install recycling bins for specific materials in communal, easy to reach areas. You will need to get the go-ahead from the local authorities and the property owners affected before moving forward. After that is sorted out, you can collect and sort the materials to sell to recycling plants.

If you are looking to start a slightly larger scale business, begin hiring employees, and provide services for larger organizations, then revisit the steps in Chapter 4. You will need to develop a good business plan to be successful with this. It is possible if you are willing to put in the work required to make it happen. You could even try a haul-away business that removes dirt and rubble from areas that are being renovated or from building sites. As long as you have a truck or a van, you could start small and grow from there.

Volunteering

Volunteering to help the environment can be such a rewarding use of your time. Not only does it help the environment, but you will be able to meet people who are like-minded and want to use their time unselfishly for the good of something greater than themselves. You will also get first-hand experience of the problems facing the environment. That could spark a passion and help you generate more ideas to make a change and make things better.

There are so many places where you can volunteer: every city will be different when it comes to volunteering opportunities. If you live near the ocean, you are almost guaranteed to have an ocean clean up initiative somewhere close by. You can visit these websites to find out what you can do to help the oceans and any volunteering opportunities near you: Trash Free Seas: Volunteer and One World One Ocean: Get Involved.

Many NGOs run on volunteers' efforts, so don't be too shy to phone or email one of them for information. Look for opportunities to do small things as well, like volunteering at a local animal shelter or conservation organization, or taking the initiative and cleaning up your local park by picking up trash. You do not even need to wait for a big organization to create a volunteering opportunity for yourself: plan something and get your friends and family to join. That is the great thing about volunteering; it can be done in any capacity.

50 Ways to Help the Environment

Small things make a big difference. We should never forget that. When we decide to change our habits and implement small changes, we can positively affect the environment in ways that we cannot see. It is always good to be mindful of what we are doing.

So here's a challenge. Below is a list of 50 things that you can do to help the environment and the planet provided by WaystoHelp (2017). How many can you do?

- Switch to energy-efficient light bulbs. That is good for both your wallet and the environment

- Make sure your computer is off at night.

- Do not rinse your dishes before washing them or tossing them into the dishwasher. Your dishes will still be clean.

- Do not preheat your oven, unless actually necessary.

- Recycle your glass.

- Opt for cloth diapers rather than disposable ones. There are environmentally friendly disposable diapers if you absolutely must use them.

- Hang your clothes up to dry instead of using the dryer.

- Have at least one meat-free day a week.

- Wash your clothes only when you have a full load and use a warm or cold setting instead of the hot water one.

- Only take napkins that you are going to use.

- Try and use all of the paper. Use the same paper to jot down multiple notes; if there is white space, you can still use it.

- Recycle your newspapers, or better yet, don't buy newspapers and just read the news online.

- Do your best not to buy new gift wrap. Get creative and use old newspapers or magazines to make your own designs.

- Don't buy bottled water: carry around a reusable bottle and fill it up with water.

- Shower rather than bathe.

- Switch the tap off when you are brushing your teeth. You do not need the water when you are brushing your teeth.

- Why not take a shower with your partner. I am sure it will be enjoyable for both of you, and you will use half the amount of water!

- Shorten your shower time. Even cutting just two minutes off it can save about ten gallons of water.

- Plant a tree. You can do this in your garden or go out and make an event of it to plant a tree every year.

- Do you have a car with cruise control? If you do then use it, you will improve your mileage and use less gas.

- Rather than buying brand new, go for second-hand items. Especially for things that don't have a long usage.

- Shop local. Local products do not need to be transported over long distances and therefore do not cause as much pollution.

- Adjust the temperature of your home. Even one degree makes a difference, and you likely won't notice.

- Use a travel mug for your hot drinks. It will keep your drinks hotter for longer, and some coffee shops will give you a small discount if you bring your own up rather than using a takeaway cup.

- Plan to do your errands in batches rather than as they pop up.

- Switch the lights off when you leave the room.

- Use a watering can instead of the hose pipe to water your plants: this way, you can concentrate on the areas that need watering. Water early in the morning to reduce water evaporation.

- Picnic with reusable cups, plates, forks, and knives. If you use disposable ones, mark each person's with their name or a different color so you won't get confused and have to keep replacing them.

- Recycle your cell phones rather than throwing them away. There are plenty of programs and places that recycle cell phones.

- Make sure you keep your vehicle well maintained. A well-maintained car is much more fuel-efficient.

- Rather than throw away wire hangers, recycle them by giving them to dry cleaners to use.

- Recycle all aluminum products.

- If it is possible, try to work from home. Even if this is just a few days a month, less travel will mean less pollution.

- Close your fireplace damper when you do not have a fire going. The open damper will suck up all the warm air in your house and cause you to waste more money on heating.

- Lessen the amount of junk mail that gets delivered to you. There are services that help you with this.

- Use matches rather than plastic lighters. The matches made from recycled paper are the best option.

- Opt-out of receiving telephone directories. Let's be honest; the online versions are much easier to navigate anyway.

- Rather than throwing away things you no longer use, why not donate them to charity or give them away to someone who could use them?

- Get your car washed professionally rather than doing it yourself. Car washes usually work out the minimum amount of water they need to wash a car since they want to save money in this regard. When we wash our cars at home, we usually use more water than is necessary.

- Use reusable carrier bags when going shopping.

- Opt for e-tickets rather than printed tickets.

- Download the software rather than buying the physical discs.

- Don't use an answering machine. It is a waste of power. Most cellphones and landlines now have voicemail services built into them.

- Use a spoon rather than a coffee stirrer to mix your coffee. Stirrers are unnecessary and are just thrown away after one use.

- Use pet-friendly, chemical-free de-icers for your driveways and other areas that get iced up after a big storm. De-icers filled with chemicals or salts are harmful to pets and can contaminate the ground and water.

- Use cotton buds with paper spindles rather than plastic ones.

- Use online means to pay your bills. That is more convenient in any case.

175

- Opt-out of receiving paper statements and go digital. It is also easier to keep track of everything on a digital platform than in a paper format. I also save important items on a thumb drive.

- Buy reusable batteries. Batteries that you throw away produce acid that corrodes in the earth if they are dumped in landfills.

- Tell others. Most people who are doing things damaging to the environment are doing so because of a lack of knowledge. Please share what you now know with your friends and family and challenge them to make a change as well.

Conclusion

I think you have found out that the magic is in you, and in the little things. It is using the things around us to create our own magic. It is being the solution and creating something beautiful in that. Sometimes magic does not have to be this far off concept but rather doing things that make your life, others' experiences, and the environment better.

My goal was to honestly fill this book with so many practical things that you can implement in your life, if not today, then soon enough. Remember when we spoke about learning in Chapter 10? Learning can only be effective when we put it into practice, and that is what I ask you to do once you put this book down. Don't let it just be knowledge that is nice to have. You have the power to change your life and change the world around you: don't you want to feel that magic?

Of course, no one is expected to do everything in this book. But could you can do one or two things to start? Perhaps you have already begun, and I hope you found a few more endeavors to consider. Every little thing can make a difference, so I ask you to take a moment and think about what stood out to you when you read through this book. Was it starting an organic garden? Or perhaps it was building an indigenous yard? Did the chapter on solar panels make you want to install them for your home as soon as possible? How about making a difference with volunteering or changing how you commute? It will probably be different for every person who picks up this book but take the time to think about what sparked something in you.

Don't think you are doing it alone, I'm here, and I'm still learning, picking up new things, and implementing them in my life. It doesn't matter when you are reading this book. You can rest assured that I am still learning, still growing, and always making changes to help make my life greener. The exciting thing is that you never get tired of it. Once you get started and begin seeing the benefits and enjoying your life in this new way, you will keep looking for those new and better ways. It is so worth it. Why do you think I am still doing it. Come and experience it with me. You will not regret it!

Gillian Carr

ABOUT THE AUTHOR

Gillian Carr is an entrepreneur, researcher, and author. She has successfully launched multiple side businesses as she raised two daughters who graduated from the University of Washington. An avid reader of United States History, she is writing various books on the subjects that have intrigued her most. Instead of being pigeon-holed into one genre, books that are being published by Gillian include a wide variety of topics. Soon to be released books include "Secrets of Inspiring Women," portraying important women from history, a startup business book "Side Hustle Magic," where some readers may shape the ideas that are revealed into a new career, healthy recipe books and more. Watch for the latest from Gillian Carr coming soon to a "bookshelf" near you!

References

Andrus, A. (2018, May 8). *Selling with Shopify: How to Build a Profitable Shopify Store*. Disruptive Advertising. https://www.disruptiveadvertising.com/ppc/e commerce/shopify-store/

Berrill, A., Card, N., Cable, J., Ferguson, D., Blanchard, T., Hughes, S., & Harper, L. (2020, February 29). *50 simple ways to make your life greener*. The Guardian. https://www.theguardian.com/environment/ 2020/feb/29/50-ways-to-green-up-your-life-save-the-planet

Boys, J. (2017, February 15). *Gardening to Save Money: 10 High-Yield Low-Cost Plants to Grow*. An Oregon Cottage. https://anoregoncottage.com/gardening-to-save-money-10-high-yield-low-cost-plants-to-grow/

Brian Clark Howard. (2018, March 21). *How to Start an Organic Garden in 9 Easy Steps*. Good Housekeeping. https://www.goodhousekeeping.com/home/g ardening/advice/g2104/organic-gardening-tips-460309/

Byczynski, L. (n.d.). *Turning a Profit by Growing Herbs | Johnny's Selected Seeds*. Johnny Seeds. Retrieved May 22, 2020, from https://www.johnnyseeds.com/growers-library/herbs/library-herbs-profit.html

Candletech (2013, August 8). *How to Make Hand-dipped Taper Candles | Candle Making Techniques*. Candletech. https://candletech.com/candle-making/how-to-make-hand-dipped-taper-candles/

Chait, J. (2019, November 20). *How You Can Sell Your Local Organic Produce to Restaurants*. The Balance Small Business. https://www.thebalancesmb.com/how-to-sell-organic-farm-goods-to-local-restaurants-2538100

Choose Energy (2019, May 5). *How does your state generate electricity?* ChooseEnergy. https://www.chooseenergy.com/data-center/electricity-sources-by-state/

Clapton, A. (2019, January 16). *How Water Filtering Helps Save Water – And The Planet*. Blue and Green Tomorrow. https://blueandgreentomorrow.com/environment/how-water-filtering-helps-save-water-and-planet/

Clark, J. (2007, November 19). *What is gray water, and can it solve the global water crisis?* HowStuffWorks. https://home.howstuffworks.com/green-living/gray-water1.htm

Compare.com. (2018, October 16). *Natural Gas Cars | Pros and Cons of CNG Powered Vehicles*.

Compare.Com.
https://www.compare.com/ways-to-save/vehicle/natural-gas-vehicles-guide

Composite Decking. (2020, March 5). *Eco Composite Decking*.
https://www.ecocompositedecking.co.uk/

Compressed Natural Gas Vehicles. (n.d.).
Cngas.Co.Uk. Retrieved May 25, 2020, from
http://www.cngas.co.uk/cngvehicles.php

Conserve Energy Future (2017, October 25). *What are 10 Different Sources of Energy?* Conserve Energy Future. https://www.conserve-energy-future.com/different-energy-sources.php

Culver, B. (2019, August 10). *Canning Preserving and Dehydrating Food Off the Grid*. An Off Grid Life. https://www.anoffgridlife.com/canning-preserving-and-dehydrating-food-off-the-grid/

Eating Well. (n.d.). *10 Steps to Water-Bath Canning*. EatingWell. Retrieved May 22, 2020, from http://www.eatingwell.com/article/15855/10-steps-to-water-bath-canning/

Elemental Green. (n.d.). *10 Steps to Rain Harvesting Sustainable Water*. ElementalGreen. Retrieved May 22, 2020, from https://elemental.green/10-steps-to-rain-harvesting-sustainable-water/

EnergySage. (2019, May 8). *How is Solar Energy Stored in 2019?* Energysage.

https://www.energysage.com/solar/solar-energy-storage/how-do-solar-batteries-work/

Epic Gardening. (2018, October 5). *Hydroponic Systems*. Epic Gardening. https://www.epicgardening.com/hydroponic-systems/

Feedvisor. (n.d.). What Is Fulfillment By Amazon (FBA)? Feedvisor. https://feedvisor.com/university/fulfillment-by-amazon/

Get Involved. (n.d.). One World One Ocean. Retrieved May 24, 2020, from http://www.oneworldoneocean.com/get-involved

Gorzelany, J. (2020, January 23). *Clean Living: These Are The 12 'Greenest' Cars For 2020*. Forbes. https://www.forbes.com/sites/jimgorzelany/2020/01/23/these-are-the-12-greenest-cars-for-2020/#63fdc242c5be

Green Education Foundation. (2018). *Rainwater Harvesting - Green Education Foundation | GEF | Sustainability Education*. Greeneducationfoundation.Org. http://www.greeneducationfoundation.org/green-building-program-sub/learn-about-green-building/1240-rainwater-harvesting.html

Greenhouse Growing. (2020, January 12). *Pros And Cons Of Hydroponic And Soil Greenhouse Growing*. Greenhouse Growing.

https://www.growingreenhouse.com/pros-and-cons-of-hydroponic-and-soil-greenhouse-growing/

Gregory, A. (2010, July 19). *Starting a Business*. The Balance Small Business. https://www.thebalancesmb.com/starting-a-small-business-4161641

Haque, T. (2029, November 20). *You Can Start a Recycling Business With a Small Investment*. The Balance Small Business. https://www.thebalancesmb.com/starting-a-recycling-business-with-minimum-investment-2877980

Harvard University. (2014, October 1). *Top 10 home energy saving tips*. Sustainability at Harvard. https://green.harvard.edu/tools-resources/green-tip/top-10-home-energy-saving-tips

Hello Wonderful. (2014, November 24). *EASY HANDMADE GOAT'S MILK CITRUS SOAPS*. Hello Wonderful. https://www.hellowonderful.co/post/easy-handmade-goat-s-milk-citrus-soaps/

Lallanilla, M. (2019, June 27). *Green Cleaning - Tips for Green Cleaning*. The Spruce. https://www.thespruce.com/tips-for-green-cleaning-1708700

Lilyquist, M. (2019, November 21). *9 Reasons to Start a Business From Your Home*. The Balance Small Business.

https://www.thebalancesmb.com/should-i-work-from-home-10-reasons-you-should-1794195

Maxwell-Gaines, C. (2018, May 5). *What are the Benefits and Advantages of Rainwater?* Innovative Water Solutions LLC. https://www.watercache.com/faqs/rainwater-harvesting-benefits

Mr. Electric. (2020). *How Does a Smart Thermostat Work?* Mr. Electric. https://mrelectric.com/blog/how-does-a-smart-thermostat-work

National Audubon Society. (2017, May 18). *Why Native Plants Matter*. Audubon. https://www.audubon.org/content/why-native-plants-matter

National Geographic. (2012, June 20). *11 of the Fastest Growing Green Jobs - National Geographic*. National Geographic. https://www.nationalgeographic.com/environment/sustainable-earth/11-of-the-fastest-growing-green-jobs/

Nissan USA. (2019). *2019 Nissan LEAF Range, Charging & Battery | Nissan USA*. Nissan USA. https://www.nissanusa.com/vehicles/electric-cars/leaf/features/range-charging-battery.html

Ocean Conservancy. (2018). *Join the wave*. Ocean Conservancy.

https://oceanconservancy.org/trash-free-seas/international-coastal-cleanup/volunteer/

Overdiep, III, J., & Shaw, A. (n.d.). *Federal and State Regulations on Selling Frozen and Dehydrated Foods.* https://www.ncrfsma.org/files/page/files/ncr_frozen_and_dehydrated_produce.pdf

Peerspace. (2019, August 27). *Here's Where to Rent Commercial Kitchen Space by the Hour.* Peerspace. https://www.peerspace.com/resources/rent-commercial-kitchen-space-by-the-hour

Peterson, S. (n.d.-a). *Dehydrating Food - How to Dry Vegetables, Peppers, Tomatoes and more.* SimplyCanning. https://www.simplycanning.com/dehydrating-vegetables.html

Peterson, S. (n.d.-b). *Dehydrating Fruit, How to dry 6 fruits for snacking and storing.* SimplyCanning. https://www.simplycanning.com/dehydrating-fruit.html

Peterson, S. (n.d.-c). *Dehydrating is the oldest (and easiest) food preservation method.* SimplyCanning. https://www.simplycanning.com/dehydrating.html

Peterson, S. (n.d.-d). *How to Dry Herbs with a simple complete step by step tutorial.* SimplyCanning.

https://www.simplycanning.com/how-to-dry-herbs.html

Pick Your Own. (n.d.-a). *Cottage Food Laws By State: How To Sell Your Homemade Foods.* Pickyourown.Org. Retrieved May 19, 2020, from https://www.pickyourown.org/CottageFoodLawsByState.htm

Pick Your Own. (n.d.-b). *Home Pressure Canner Directions: How They Work, Instructions and Tips to Using Them!* Pickyourown.Org. Retrieved May 22, 2020, from https://pickyourown.org/pressurecanners.htm

Pilon, A. (2017, August 14). *25 Tips for Small Businesses Selling at Farmers Markets.* Small Business Trends. https://smallbiztrends.com/2017/08/selling-at-farmers-markets.html

Pinola, M. (2015, May 20). *This Graphic Shows the Best Air-Cleaning Plants, According to NASA.* Lifehacker.Com. https://lifehacker.com/this-graphic-shows-the-best-air-cleaning-plants-accord-1705307836

Popovich, N. (2018, December 24). *How Does Your State Make Electricity?* The New York Times. https://www.nytimes.com/interactive/2018/12/24/climate/how-electricity-generation-changed-in-your-state.html

ProFlowers. (2016, November 16). *The Greenhouse Gardening Guide - ProFlowers Blog*. ProFlowers Blog. https://www.proflowers.com/blog/greenhous e-gardening-guide

Radley, R. (2019, June 10). *13 of the best electric bikes for 2019: all you need to know about e-bikes*. Cycling Weekly. https://www.cyclingweekly.com/group-tests/best-electric-bikes-need-know-e-bikes-322613

Ray, J. (2015, October 4). *7 Ways to Sell Your Produce to Local Restaurants*. Hobby Farms. https://www.hobbyfarms.com/7-ways-to-sell-your-produce-to-local-restaurants-2/

Richter, C. (2007, October 9). *Commercial Herb Production and Marketing*. Richters. https://www.richters.com/show.cgi?page=Qa ndA/Commercial/20071009-1.html

Roizen, B. (2019, December 17). *How to Sell on eBay & Realistically Make Money (2020)*. The BigCommerce Blog. https://www.bigcommerce.com/blog/selling-on-ebay-for-beginners/#who-is-selling-on-ebay

Sanchez, B. (2019, March 6). *Is composite decking worth the extra cost?* Shorty and Slim Garden Decking. https://shortyandslim.com/is-composite-decking-worth-the-extra-cost/

Sandhu, J. (2019, June 28). *Which new solar panel technologies will revolutionize energy production?* Solar Reviews. https://www.solarreviews.com/blog/solar-panel-technologies-that-will-revolutionize-energy-production

Sfgate. (n.d.). *Organic Vs. Non-Organic Plants.* Home Guides | SF Gate. https://homeguides.sfgate.com/organic-vs-nonorganic-plants-86063.html

Solar Reviews. (2019). *Solar panel cost 2019: by state, by system size and by panel manufacturer.* Solarreviews.Com. https://www.solarreviews.com/solar-panels/solar-panel-cost/

Sound Dietitians. (2018, October 21). *Food Preservation – Canning, Dehydrating, & Freezing.* SOUND DIETITIANS LLC. https://www.sounddietitians.com/blog/food-preservation-canning-dehydrating-freezing

Sylvia, T. (2020, March 6). *How the new generation of 500 W panels will shape the solar industry.* Pv Magazine International. https://www.pv-magazine.com/2020/03/06/how-the-new-generation-of-500-watt-panels-will-shape-the-solar-industry/

The All State Blog. (2018, May 14). *Does Color Affect the Temperature of Your Home?* The Allstate Blog. https://www.allstate.com/blog/home-color-material-affect-temperature/

The Lung Health Institute. (2016, July 15). *Lung Institute | Top 5 Plants for Increasing Oxygen*. Lung Institute. https://lunginstitute.com/blog/top-5-plants-for-increasing-oxygen/

Tilley, N. (n.d.). *Growing A Vertical Vegetable Garden*. Gardeningknowhow.Com. Retrieved May 22, 2020, from https://www.gardeningknowhow.com/edible/vegetables/vgen/growing-a-vertical-vegetable-garden.htm

United States Environmental Protection Agency. (2020, March 10). *Power Profiler*. US EPA. https://www.epa.gov/energy/power-profiler#/

U.S. Department of Energy. (n.d.). *Alternative Fuels Data Center: Natural Gas Fueling Station Locations*. Alternative Fuels Data Center. Retrieved May 24, 2020, from https://afdc.energy.gov/fuels/natural_gas_lo cations.html#/find/nearest?fuel=CNG

Wallin, C. (2012, September 12). *Ten Most Profitable Herbs To Grow*. Headstart Publishing. https://headstartpublishing.com/ten-most-profitable-herbs-to-grow/

Wallin, Craig. (2019a, May 18). *How to Start a Trash Removal Business for Just $400*. Haul Away Cash. https://www.haulawaycash.com/how-to-start-a-haul-away-business-for-just-400/

Wallin, Craig. (2019b, August 20). *Sell Your Harvest Direct to Local Grocery Stores*. Profitable Plants Digest. https://www.profitableplantsdigest.com/sell-your-harvest-direct-to-local-grocery-stores/

Ward, S. (2020, February 3). *6 Steps to Starting a Home-Based Business That Will Succeed*. The Balance Small Business. https://www.thebalancesmb.com/how-to-start-a-home-based-business-that-will-succeed-2948192

WaystoHelp. (2017). *50 Ways to Help the Planet - Save Our Environment and Planet Earth*. 50 WaystoHelp. https://www.50waystohelp.com/

wikiHow. (n.d.). *How to Start a Recycling Business*. WikiHow. Retrieved May 24, 2020, from https://www.wikihow.com/Start-a-Recycling-Business

World Population Review. (2020, April 6). *States Where It Is Illegal To Collect Rainwater 2020*. World Population Review. https://worldpopulationreview.com/states/states-where-it-is-illegal-to-collect-rainwater/

Image References

All images sourced from https://unsplash.com/

Except Seattle photo chapter 6 courtesy Town and Country Markets/ CB Nuts